The Manager's Pocke...

Providing Performance Feedback to Non-Exempt Employees

Peter R. Garber

HRD Press, Inc. • Amherst, MA

Published by: HRD Press, Inc.
22 Amherst Road
Amherst, MA 01002
800-822-2801 (U.S. and Canada)
413-253-3488
413-253-3490 (fax)
www.hrdpress.com

ISBN 978-1-61014-423-0

Production services by Jean Miller
Cover design by Eileen Klockars
Editorial services by

— Contents —

— Introduction —

There is no question that the non-exempt employees you supervise play an extremely important role in contributing to the overall success of your organization. These are people who typically perform the tasks that most directly impact your customers. They may perform the jobs that keep your operation running efficiently or they may be in direct contact with your customers, often face-to-face, providing services to the customer. Helping these key employees perform their jobs to the best of their abilities is a good investment in both your time and your organization's resources. There may be few other things you can do in your role as a supervisor or manager of non-exempt employees that ultimately can have such a big impact on the bottom-line performance of your organization.

Unfortunately, this is also the group that often "falls between the cracks" when it comes to providing effective performance feedback concerning their job performance. There are many reasons why this might occur in an organization, which will be discussed in more detail later in this book. However, the most common reason is typically that managers and supervisors today feel they don't have the time in their busy work schedules to provide performance feedback to employees. But somehow finding or making the time can ultimately make your job more productive as well as easier. You can help your employees better perform their jobs and feel more appreciated and recognized for the good work they perform every day. This feedback can also allow them to better understand how they can improve their performance in the future.

Your employees want feedback on their performance if it is presented in a supportive, fair, and objective manner. This is one of the most important challenges that you as a supervisor or manager will face in your job. Think about your own personal experiences receiving performance feedback from your supervisors throughout your career. Were you always satisfied with the quality of this feedback or the commitment from your supervisors to provide you with the best feedback possible to help you grow and develop in your position? The honest answer is you probably were disappointed at times concerning the performance feedback you received from some of your supervisors. Now, think about some the best performance feedback you received. Think about the difference that made in your overall performance on your job. Your goal should be to emulate those supervisors when it comes to providing feedback to those who report to you. Think about what a difference this could make in their performance.

This book will help you meet this challenge as well as provide your non-exempt employees with the feedback they need to perform their jobs to the best of their abilities. However, the concepts presented in this book can also be applicable when providing performance feedback to your exempt employees as well. The basic principles for effectively providing this feedback are essentially the same, regardless of the level of an employee's position in the organization.

Providing effective performance feedback, no doubt, has been a challenge since the first time people started working for one another and bosses struggled to find ways to provide this feedback. Many of the principles and concepts presented in this book are indeed timeless and universal and based on years of experience working with both supervisors and employees in trying to find the best ways to communicate feedback. In the final analysis, what is most important is that you are committed to providing the most accurate, candid, constructive performance feedback to your employees. It many ways, it really is as simple as that. This is an area in which effort is probably the most important factor in your success. What is most important is not whether you are the most skilled provider of performance feedback but rather, most important is your commitment to provide this feedback to your employees in a way that can truly help them perform their jobs better in the future.

Although the focus of this book is on providing performance feedback, it is also important to think about what it is like to receive feedback as well. Again, thinking about your own experiences receiving performance feedback should help guide you in this area. But receptivity to feedback on performance can be an issue, regardless of the effort made to present the feedback in a manner the employee can accept. There can be many reasons why employees might not be receptive to receiving performance feedback, such as past poor experiences or trust factors that inhibit the process. If there are problems in the working relationship between an employee and his or her supervisor, this process will be even more challenging and probably less effective. However, even under these circumstances, it is important, perhaps even more so, to provide the best performance feedback to your employees. In fact, this can be a positive step toward building or rebuilding trust.

In recent years, there has been considerable focus on finding alternative methods for providing performance feedback to the classic format of a supervisor and employee sitting down and discussing the employee's performance and providing some type of overall performance rating. Many organizations become disenchanted with their current performance feedback processes and systems, believing that they are ineffective in changing or improving performance. They hear complaints from their employees about what is perceived to be an unfair system or one based more on favoritism than actual performance. Employees may become legitimately concerned about the potential of becoming "labeled" according to the formal performance levels which, once given, may seem virtually impossible to change despite their hard work and efforts to do so. Even managers and supervisors may voice concerns about the ineffectiveness of the existing performance feedback process currently in place within the organization. They might feel that it does little else but cause resentment from their direct reports regarding the ratings they receive. These are legitimate concerns and might be relevant to your organization.

In one organization, the top management of the company became frustrated with the constant complaints by managers and employees regarding the effectiveness of its performance management process. It seemed that a tremendous amount of effort was expended, requiring supervisors to provide performance evaluation ratings to employees with little actual benefit expected. This created much resentment and hard feelings on the part of the employees, who were dissatisfied with how they were being rated. Previously, the company had moved from a performance rating system that included five formal evaluation levels, expanded by the use of plus or minus additional ratings which could be applied for each level, resulting in at least nine different performance evaluation levels being utilized. With so many different levels of performance, there wasn't much distinction between these ratings. Making matters worse, the company had no distribution requirements for each of the ratings. With no controls in place, over time, ratings tended to gravitate toward the higher ratings, as supervisors found it easier to present a higher rating to their employees.

In a reactionary mode, the company moved to a three-level performance rating system of Needs Improvement, Meets Requirements, and Exceeds Requirements, with the requirement that at least 70% of employees fall into the Meets Requirements rating. This new system did little to address the concerns that employees had about their ratings. With the majority of employees now expected to be rated as Meets Requirements, this exacerbated the problem with the system. Even supervisors disliked now being limited in providing the higher performance ratings to more of their employees.

In total frustration, the company adopted a performance feedback system with no performance ratings, believing that this would eliminate the churn and dissatisfaction of employees concerning the ratings they received from their supervisors. What the company quickly discovered was that there was an inherent need for some type of performance evaluation ratings. Without having these ratings, they found they had no way to differentiate great performance from good performance and reward good performance properly. There was also no objective measure to identify employees with the top talent.

It wasn't long before the company had reinstated a performance rating system, this time focused on training supervisors how to provide fair and accurate performance evaluations to employees. Although not everyone was totally satisfied with the new system, it did provide the company with the ability to administer a fair and objective performance feedback program, allowing supervisors to give employees feedback on their true level of performance. These concepts will be further explained in the upcoming chapters of this book.

The debate concerning what is the best performance feedback system is one that will likely be ongoing. What is most important is what works best in your organization. However, the basis of any system, regardless if it includes assigning performance levels in some manner or a supervisor/employee feedback meeting, must be based on honesty. As long as supervisors sincerely endeavor to provide helpful, constructive feedback, the performance feedback system will be successful in meeting its goals. The approach to providing performance feedback that is presented in this book is more of a "back-to-basics" approach. It is the author's belief that there really is no substitute to a supervisor or manager sitting down with an employee, face-to-face, and providing honest feedback based on that employee's job performance and engaging in a meaningful dialog about their career goals and aspirations.

−1−

The Importance of Performance Feedback

Why provide performance feedback to employees? This is a fair question and one that may often be debated by skeptics of many existing performance feedback processes. Employees may have good reason for their skepticism if past performance feedback processes failed them in some manner, such as if the quality or consistency of the performance feedback was lacking, their supervisor didn't do a very good job in meeting their expectations or was unfair or biased against them in some way and did not give them the performance rating they deserved.

The reality is that most employees *do* want to receive feedback on their performance. It is important to them, and the absence of receiving performance feedback is often a source of complaint and discontent among employees. They intuitively understand that receiving effective performance feedback from their supervisor is key to their continued success within the organization and to their growth and development on the job.

The following are just some of the many reasons why performance feedback is necessary and important to your employees.

1. **Performance feedback lets employees know how they are performing on the job.** This is perhaps the most important benefit. Everyone needs feedback about their performance on the job. Without this feed-

back, employees will not know if they are meeting the expectations of their supervisor and others in the organization. They might end up guessing as to whether or not they are performing their jobs correctly until some event occurs, often something negative, such as a costly problem or mistake that ends up forcing a discussion with their supervisor about their performance. A far more positive and proactive approach would be one in which employees receive regular feedback from their supervisor on all aspects of their performance. It gives the employee a better understanding of how he or she is currently perceived by their manager or supervisor concerning job performance. In some cases, it might also be important to provide feedback to employees about how they are perceived by others in the organization, especially those with whom they are in regular contact as they perform their jobs.

This last point is particularly important for the employee to understand. An employee's career growth and development are not usually solely determined by his or her supervisor. Other key decision-makers in the organization may also have a say in this matter. In most organizations, ratings are reviewed by a group of decision-makers to review the performance rating recommendations of individual supervisors. This is sometimes called a *Leveling Committee.* This function is necessary to ensure that everyone is being evaluated according to the same standards, as some supervisors might be more inclined to give higher ratings than others. In most performance management systems, there are limitations on the number of employees who can receive the highest ratings that typically also earn higher annual raises. This is necessary to avoid *rating inflation* in which disproportionate numbers of employees received the highest ratings, which actually devalues the relative worth and meaning of the ratings for everyone, including those who truly deserve them based on their performance. Thus, it is important that employees make a positive impression on their direct supervisor as well as those key decision-makers in the organization who may ultimately have a say in how their performance is rated at the end of this process. This is something that supervisors should make sure their employees understand, and they should provide them with feedback on how they might be presently perceived (fairly or unfairly) by others in the organization. Some employees might not want to hear this because they feel that their supervisor alone should make the decision concerning their final performance evaluation.

2. **It provides a fair and accurate evaluation to each employee about his/her performance.** One of the greatest challenges in providing performance feedback is to ensure that the process is fair. More importantly, your *employees* must feel that the process is fair. One of the best ways to ensure fairness is to consistently adhere to an established performance feedback process that sets forth required steps and standards to be followed throughout the year. It is also important that this feedback is accurate. Employees might not always agree with the feedback they receive, therefore, there must be a basis for the evaluation. Providing documentation, personal experiences, and other examples helps validate the feedback. Giving vague or unclear reasons to an employee concerning his or her performance rating will make it much less likely that feedback will be perceived as fair. For example, think about the following dialog between a supervisor and an employee during a performance feedback meeting:

Supervisor: I am rating you lower this year because I don't think you are doing as good a job as you did in the past.

Employee: I don't understand. I do the same thing every day I come to work and that hasn't changed over the past year. This is the first time you have even mentioned this to me. Could you give me some specific examples of what you mean?

Supervisor: Well, this is just something that I have observed over the past year. I can't be any more specific than that. I can just tell when someone is doing a good job and when they are not.

Employee: That doesn't give me much to work on if I ever expect to get a better rating next year.

Supervisor: Well, you need to think about what you can do to improve your performance so we don't have to have this same discussion then.

Just think about how this employee must have felt as he left this performance evaluation meeting. He wouldn't have a clue as to why he was being rated lower this performance year or what to focus on to improve his supposed lower performance. Unfortunately, this is the type of vague, nonspecific performance feedback that many employees receive.

3. **Provides guidance on individual needs for career development.** The topic that most employees are interested in hearing about from their supervisors is what career opportunities might lay ahead for them in the future. Unfortunately, this is a topic that may

not always be covered in performance feedback sessions. This might occur because the supervisor is focused on the employee's current performance during the meeting, or there might not be enough time to allow for a career development discussion. It might also be that discussing an employee's career development is not part of the organization's design for the performance feedback process. Employees want this feedback and will often leave disappointed if they do not discuss their performance or receive guidance on their future career possibilities.

This feedback, or lack thereof, is probably what they share with their family and friends when talking about their most recent performance feedback session. Too often, this critically important part of the meeting is cut short due to lack of time allowed, as illustrated by the following example:

Supervisor: I'm afraid that we're almost out of time in this meeting and we both need to get back out on the floor. I think we did have a good discussion on your performance last year.

Employee: Yes, I agree that it was a good discussion, but I was hoping we could have a chance to discuss any career opportunities that might exist for me in the future before we ended today.

Supervisor: That is something we need to discuss, but like I said, we're out of time today. We need to find another time to sit down and discuss this.

Employee: Okay. I'll wait to hear from you to set something up.

Obviously, in this example, discussing future career opportunities was very important to the employee and he was disappointed that it wasn't covered during the meeting. What kind of message do you think the supervisor sent to the employee concerning how important this part of the discussion was to him? The fact that the employee's career development wasn't covered during the meeting probably already answered this question. Be sure that you include a discussion about an employee's career goals and development in every performance feedback meeting that you have, as it will likely be the most important part of the discussion. A good tip is to actually begin with the career discussion before getting into the performance feedback part of the session, to emphasize its importance and to ensure that adequate time is spent on this aspect of the meeting.

4. **It identifies areas for improvement that otherwise might not have been addressed.** It is important that employees receive feedback not only concerning what they are doing well on their jobs, but also areas that need improvement. This topic will be discussed in further detail later in this book. Too often, this is an area that is not always addressed during performance feedback meetings. There sometimes are "unspoken expectations" between supervisors and employees that are never clearly identified or communicated. Supervisors often get frustrated with an employee's performance, but fail to tell the employee about his or her deficiencies. When a supervisor does not address performance deficiencies, it is not only unfair to the employee, but does not help him or her improve in the future. Select a private, confidential setting to discuss often potentially sensitive issues relating to

an employee's performance. Never discuss these problems in front of other employees or peers.

5. **Reinforces good and/or excellent performance.** Similar to not addressing poor performance, not addressing good and/or excellent performance can be just as problematic. Many employees work hard to excel in their jobs and their efforts need to be recognized and reinforced. This also motivates employees to repeat such great performance in the future. Many employees feel that they are just not being recognized or appreciated by their supervisor for their accomplishments on the job. As one employee stated: "I would like my boss to say thank you to me just once for everything I do on my job!" Think about what would cause someone to consider how much he or she was appreciated on the job. A lack of feedback about an employee's good performance can be just as detrimental as a lack of feedback concerning poor performance. Neither addresses the performance level being demonstrated.

6. **Identifies top performers and top talent in the organization.** It is important that there be a system in place to identify top performers and top talent, for they are the individuals who often contribute the most in helping to achieve your organization's goals. They are key to the future success of the organization. Developing these top performers and talented individuals should be a key responsibility of every supervisor. Providing developmental opportunities for this group can yield great payback in terms of having talented individuals ready and available as future opportunities exist within your organization.

7. **Creates a written record of an employee's past performance.** There are many reasons why it is important that there be a documented record of an employee's past performance history. It can be useful when considering the employee for a promotion, a different job assignment, or other development opportunity. It might also be important to support a low rating or negative performance feedback if there are performance problems resulting in the need to consider disciplinary or other adverse employment actions.

Types of Performance Feedback

There are two types of performance feedback:

- **Formal:** Documented annual/semiannual performance review

- **Informal:** Day-to-day communication and feedback about performance

Which do you think is the most important factor in determining performance? The answer is that each is important, providing both immediate feedback and an overview of each employee's performance over time. A good question would be if you could only have one or the other, which would you pick that would have the greatest impact on employee performance?

There may be no absolute right or wrong answer to this question, but it still serves as an interesting discussion point. The focus of this book is more on the formal feedback process, but there is no diminishing the importance of informal day-to-day coaching, which gives employees the frequent feedback and support needed to help them perform their jobs on an ongoing basis. These day-to-day communications are a good way to continue to reinforce the feedback received during the most recent formal performance feedback review.

Feedback for Continuous Learning

Feedback is important for growth, development, and continual learning in life. The purpose of feedback is to promote learning and thus enhance performance. There are four levels of feedback an employee might receive from his or her supervisor:

- Level 1: No feedback
- Level 2: Only positive feedback
- Level 3: Only negative feedback
- Level 4: Balanced feedback

Each of these four levels is more effective than the previous one.

Level 1 – No Feedback

The first (and worst) level of feedback is actually receiving no feedback at all. Believe it or not, this level exists in many organizations, most likely occurring more often than might be expected. Think about some of the many problems created if an employee receives no performance feedback.

There are many reasons why this situation exists, which are discussed in the next chapter. But the quick answer is that providing performance feedback to employees is not easy—it is hard work.

Blindfolded Golf. Feedback is important in any activity we engage in, even when pursuing our favorite pastimes. What would it be like if you received no feedback when you pursued some of your favorite activities? For instance, imagine what it would be like if a golfer received no feedback on his performance. What if every time he swung the club, someone blindfolded him so he couldn't see where the ball landed and was not allowed to keep score on each hole? What if the results of the round of golf were mailed to him at the end of the year instead of given immediately after the round was played? Do you think that this golfer would be able to improve his game without receiving any feedback concerning his play? Do you think that he would still enjoy the game as much under these circumstances?

If you are a poor golfer, you may be thinking it might be better to not see the results of your performance! But part of what makes golf enjoyable and challenging is receiving feedback right away after each swing. Either the golfer sees the results of swinging the club properly or the consequences of not performing this correctly.

Level 2 – Only Positive Feedback

What if an employee only receives positive feedback, assuming that there are negatives to be discussed? At first, this might sound like a desirable situation. But would this really be a beneficial way to provide feedback to employees? If employees don't hear about those aspects of their job performance that are lacking, they won't be able to address these problems and grow in their jobs and careers. In many ways, a supervisor does an injustice to the employee by focusing only on the positive performance and not communicating where the employee needs to improve. It is important for employees to hear candid, honest, and thoughtful feedback on those aspects of their job performance that might need improvement. Often, feedback that is hardest to hear can ultimately be the most beneficial to an employee's growth and development on the job.

Level 3 – Only Negative Feedback

What happens if an employee only receives negative feedback? This is also a common occurrence in many workplaces. This situation creates problems, such as negatively affecting the employee's self-esteem, creating an uncomfortable work environment, and potentially creating a poor working relationship between employee and supervisor. This type of work environment would certainly cause employees to not look forward to receiving performance feedback from their supervisor. Only receiving negative feedback creates a default performance feedback system which could be best described as:

> *"If you don't hear anything, you are doing just fine. But if you screw up, we'll let you know!"*

Level 4 – Balanced Feedback

This is the optimum level of feedback an employee should receive from his or her supervisor. Balanced feedback means that the employee receives both positive and negative feedback on how he or she can improve performance.

The ratio of positive to negative feedback should be determined by the employee's actual performance, but there should be much more positive than negative feedback presented to the employee, preferably at a 4 to 1 ratio (meaning that there should be 4 instances of positive feedback to every 1 instance of negative feedback). Usually during a performance evaluation, an employee's strengths are presented first and followed by any areas that could be improved upon. These should be reviewed in a constructive and developmental way.

What Are You Really Evaluating When You Provide Feedback to Employees?

There are a number of factors that contribute to the overall work performance of your employees. Shown below are the factors of an employee's skills, attitudes, and behaviors, as these relate to the individual's overall job performance. Understanding what contributes to this overall performance is key to you as a manager or supervisor, especially if you expect to influence performance. Failure to recognize or appreciate any single factor in this model might create a gap in accurately evaluating an employee's overall performance. Exploring each of these factors can help you better understand an employee's overall needs concerning feedback on his or her performance or what to address to help employees improve their performance in the future.

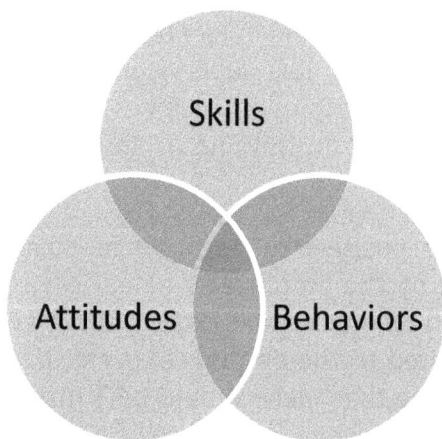

Which is the most important factor in determining an employee's overall job performance: Skills, Attitudes, or Behaviors?

Are the skills an employee brings to the job most important? Obviously, any employee must have the prerequisite skills (including innate skills, trainable skills, and

any related job experience) necessary to perform his or her job acceptably. But are skills alone enough to ensure that this level of performance is achieved or exceeded?

Also critically important is one's attitude about the job. How big a part do you think attitude towards a job plays when it comes to an employee's overall job performance, including their relationship with their supervisor? How much do fairness issues (either perceived or real) come into play as they relate to an employee's attitude about his or her job? An employee's job attitude can be influenced by many different factors. As their manager or supervisor, you may have little or no influence on these factors, while on others you may have a great deal. The relationship that an employee has with their supervisor is one of the most important determining factors in that person's attitude about their job. The better your working relationship with those who report to you, the better their attitude will be.

Finally, an employee's behaviors on the job can have a huge impact on his or her job performance. If someone has an attitude problem for whatever reason, all the skills that individual brings to the job could be overshadowed by their poor attitude, which may then result in nonproductive behaviors on the job. Job behaviors are influenced by a person's attitude, experiences, expectations, goals, etc. Behavior is what everyone sees and often defines the person as well as his or her performance.

Ultimately, it is the intersection of all three of these factors—skills, attitudes, and behaviors—that will determine an employee's overall job performance. Each factor plays a critical part and each influences the other two factors. The question you should be asking yourself is how much influence do you have in affecting each of these factors for your employees? Most likely the answer is more than you might presently realize.

Chapter Review

1. How do you feel your job could be made easier and more productive by providing more effective performance feedback to the non-exempt employees who report to you?

2. What support do you feel you might need in order to improve the performance feedback you provide to your direct reports? How can you best gain this support? Who should you go to in order to get this support?

3. Which of the seven reasons for providing performance feedback do you feel is most important? Which do you feel you do the best job at when providing performance feedback to your employees? Which do you feel you need to improve?

4. Which do you think is most important in determining an employee's overall job performance: skills, attitudes, or behaviors? Why? How much influence do you feel you have on each of these performance factors?

Performance Feedback Tips

- Consider providing performance feedback to be one of your most important responsibilities as a supervisor or manager.

- Commit the time both in preparation and presenting performance feedback to ensure that you have done the best you can do to deliver meaningful feedback to your direct reports.

- Think of spending more time on performance feedback as an investment in your employees' future job performance.

Action Planner

Think about a supervisor you have had either presently or in the past that you thought did a great job in providing feedback on your performance. What did he or she do that made this experience so valuable and memorable to you? How can you emulate this supervisor in providing more effective (and memorable) performance feedback to your non-exempt employees? What would you do differently to meet this challenge?

— 2 —
Performance Feedback Challenges

There are many challenges to creating an effective performance feedback process. Identifying these challenges is the first step to creating a more effective process for providing this feedback to your employees. The following are some of the most common problems with typical performance feedback systems.

- **A performance feedback system might not exist or is not administered consistently.** A formal established performance feedback system or process may not be currently in place in the organization or, if one does exist, it is not followed consistently. However, it is likely that some form of performance feedback or evaluation process has been put in place in most organizations but it is also likely that it has been allowed to become outdated and is no longer particularly relevant to the current organization.

- **Lack of enforced performance feedback process by the organization.** Following up on the last point, there needs to be a mandated formal performance feedback process established and enforced in some way by the organization to realistically expect a consistently followed process. Like it or not, this is not something that will likely occur without a mandate by the organization. The goal should be to make the process meaningful and beneficial to both supervisors and employees so that they will begin to appreciate the value of engaging in this process.

- **Quality of the dialog/discussion between supervisor and employee concerning job performance.** It isn't enough just to mandate that performance feedback meetings by the organization occur regularly. These need to be quality discussions between a supervisor and employee that include meaningful dialog. This book is designed to help you, as a supervisor or manager, improve the quality of your discussions about performance.

- **Lack of connection to reward systems.** It is possible to have to an effective performance feedback process that is not connected to the organization's reward systems—raises, bonuses, promotions, etc. However, it might make the performance feedback process less effective or less consequential. It is best to connect the feedback process to the reward system to ensure that employees understand how they stand with respect to qualifying for these rewards as well as the rational for these discussions.

- **Perceived (or real) biases.** Perhaps one of the greatest challenges is that employees sometimes feel that the process is biased against them and that they are not being fairly evaluated by their supervisor. When this occurs, there is far less value to the process, as employees will tend to dismiss any negative feedback received as just another example of the "boss doesn't like me" syndrome that they believe exists. Every effort should be taken to ensure that there is no bias in your feedback process and that the information presented is based solely on the employee's performance and no other factors. This would be a good discussion topic between a supervisor and an employee if such feelings exist.

- **Lack of visibility of process.** Finally, it is important to make sure that the process is frequently discussed and visible to everyone. This should be part of the culture of the organization and employees should be well aware that they will be participating in this process on a regular basis.

Feedback is Hard Work, But Worth the Effort

Providing effective feedback is hard work, but worth the effort. There are many reasons why this is often one of the most challenging assignments you might face as part of your job as a supervisor or manager. As mentioned in the introduction, finding the time to do this well can be a real challenge. You have many competing priorities for your time, a number of which may seem mutually exclusive; to have one, you have to forsake another. But there are few, if any, other responsibilities you have that potentially can have as big an impact as spending the time necessary to ensure that your employees are receiving effective performance feedback. However, just committing the time to complete this responsibility is not the only challenge. Sometimes, determining what feedback to provide to employees is a challenge in itself. The performance level of many employees might not always be clear. Or an employee might be excelling in one aspect of his or her job but is deficient in others. Determining an overall performance assessment in these cases can be difficult.

Limited Rewards Lead to Forced Choices

It is necessary to have limited rewards in a performance feedback process, otherwise, if you overinflate the ratings, there will be no perceived value placed on the highest levels of performance. Perhaps even more challenging is the fact that providing performance evaluations which assign a certain level of performance for employees involves making forced choices, and often these choices are not clear in a limited rewards process.

You might find yourself in the predicament of believing more of your employees than the system will permit deserve a higher or the highest performance rating, but you are restricted to only giving these highest ratings to a certain smaller percentage of your workgroup. You realize that some employees who work hard and produce good results might receive an overall rating less than they expected or feel that they deserve. This can create morale and even motivational problems during the next performance feedback cycle.

Some may argue that having limited rewards is actually demotivating to employees, particularly those who don't receive the performance ratings they feel they deserve. Why not have a performance feedback process in which there are no rating levels, just feedback? As mentioned in the example from the introduction, there would be

- nothing that differentiates levels of performance,

- no basis for providing rewards to motivate top performing employees,

- nothing to identify high-potential employees for future development,

- an adverse affect on other employment processes dependent on a performance rating system.

Although it might seem to be less bureaucratic to eliminate these processes altogether, they do serve a necessary purpose. Ultimately, do you think it would be fair to have a process in which everyone received the same rating or no rating at all? Is just having a dialog between a supervisor and an employee concerning his or her job performance enough without assigning a rating to performance? These are questions that every organization must ask itself to find a system that works best for it.

Difficult Discussions

On the other end of the performance spectrum is addressing issues of poor performance. This discussion is not necessarily confined to those who might be considered poor performers. Almost everyone has certain deficiencies or performance areas that could be improved. Discussing these areas with someone is typically a difficult and uncomfortable task for any supervisor. They involve addressing sensitive and uncomfortable performance issues that many, if not most, managers and supervisors would rather avoid. However, actually having these types of discussions can result in significantly improved performance. Often, addressing performance issues rather than ignoring them can result in correcting the problem; particularly when the employee was not aware there was an issue with performance.

The most important thing to remember when discussing performance problems is making clear what you expect of the employee. This eliminates the excuse (valid or not) that "I was never told I was not performing to your expectations." Having these difficult conversations should take this excuse off the table.

It might also be uncomfortable giving constructive criticism to good or top performers concerning aspects of their performance that could be improved. Accepting the challenge of taking on these difficult discussions with employees on all performance levels can become one the most beneficial things you can do to help your direct reports perform their jobs to the best of their abilities.

Seven Common Problems with Performance Feedback

The following are some of the most common problems that occur when providing performance feedback. Each one in itself can significantly impact the overall effectiveness of the performance feedback an employee receives as well as the perceived credibility of the process to your workforce.

1. **Not addressing or documenting poor performance.** The first and most common problem is a supervisor or manager not addressing and documenting poor performance. This sends a mixed signal to the employee that their current level of performance is acceptable and doesn't address the performance issues that exist. This also fails to create documentation that would be necessary to take action to correct these issues in the event that such actions would need to be defended at a later date.

2. **New supervisor evaluates employee differently than previous supervisor (usually worse).** Sometimes referred to as the "new supervisor syndrome," this situation occurs when a new supervisor or manager takes over a function and addresses performance issues that might not have been addressed in the past. If this is an accurate and fair assessment, then there is no problem. However, there is now a contradictory history of this individual's performance, having been rated in the past as an acceptable performer. In this case, accurate current documentation would prove even more important to sup-

port the lower evaluation in spite of there being a past record of the employee's acceptable performance.

3. **An employee with a history of top ratings receives a lower rating without adequate documentation or explanation from the supervisor.** Sometimes an employee with a history of top ratings receives a lower rating from their same supervisor for any number of legitimate reasons. Without providing the employee with clear and specific feedback as to why this occurred, they will be confused and frustrated, believing that they performed at the same level during this current performance cycle as in the past, but yet now is receiving a lower rating.

4. **Perception that someone newly promoted into a new job can't receive a top performance rating that year.** There seems to be an "unwritten rule" in some organizations that if an employee has been promoted during the past year, he or she shouldn't be eligible for a higher performance rating that same year, especially if a raise accompanies the promotion. This happens because a supervisor or manager, in the spirit of giving, wants to allow employees who do not normally receive the higher ratings to have a chance for higher performance ratings, even if only for this one year. It is doubtful that there is any such official rule or policy in their organization, but often it is believed that one exists, perhaps mostly on the basis of past practices.

5. **Giving a raise or a performance bonus to someone who hasn't earned it for reasons other than performance.** Similarly, you might hear that the reason why an employee with average or below average performance receives a raise, bonus, or some other compensation award was because the

supervisor was trying to allow other employees who do not normally receive these awards to increase their base salaries more significantly than normal annual raises will permit. This is obviously something that should not be done for a number of reasons, one being that it might create an inaccurate and contradictory record of an employees' poor performance.

6. **Documented performance and ratings are not consistent with employment actions being requested.** Related to the last point, often the documented performance ratings are inconsistent with an adverse employment action that a supervisor or manager recommends concerning a particular employee. Again, without supporting documentation, this can create a problem if the action is the basis of a claim made against the company, especially if it results in a termination. For example, if an employee has a record of documented good or adequate performance and a supervisor is trying to make the case for discipline or even termination based on this employee's current and overall past performance history, there will be a problem or disconnect between the record and the adverse employment actions being considered. This is just another reason to make sure that you are always providing accurate feedback to your employees, especially when there are performance problems to be addressed and documented.

7. **Transferring an employee with performance problems rather than addressing the issue.** Finally, supervisors and managers shouldn't transfer an employee to another position to avoid dealing with their performance issues. This would be made even worse if the supervisor gave the employee a better rating than deserved in order to make him or her a

more attractive candidate for another position. This is another reason why it is important to address, not ignore, poor performance. You wouldn't want someone doing this to you and you shouldn't do this to any other supervisor or manager.

Dealing with Different Performance Levels

Typically, there are three levels of performance that you can expect to find in most organizations and groups of employees. These may be described using different terminology or there might be more performance rating levels in your organization, but essentially it comes down to these three performance levels:

- Top performers
- Middle performers
- Low performers

Generally, in a normal distribution of performance ratings, you can expect to find that about 20 percent of your employees are top performers, 70 percent are middle performers, and 10 percent are low performers.

Which do you think is most difficult to manage? The answer may not always be the same, as each performance level presents its own challenges. You need to have different performance feedback strategies for different levels of performers. The following chapters of this book will help you develop more effective strategies for dealing effectively with each of these levels of performance.

Chapter Review

1. Do you believe that your employees perceive the performance feedback process in your organization to be fair and unbiased? How can you influence this perception?

2. Of the seven common problems with performance feedback presented in this chapter, which do you find most challenging and why?

3. Which performance level do you think is the most difficult to manage and provide effective performance feedback for?

4. What is the distribution of performance ratings you give to employees when providing performance feedback? Does it follow the common distribution of 20 percent top performers, 70 percent middle performers, and 10 percent low performers recommended distribution?

Performance Feedback Tips

- Look at the history of your employees' performance evaluations and ratings to see if they have been consistent with how you see each employee's current performance. If there are changes that you are contemplating, make sure that there are specific reasons for these changes which can be explained to employees receiving different ratings.

- Be prepared for some employees to question their performance ratings during your performance feedback meetings with them. Do not engage in any discussions concerning other employees' performance evaluations. Instead, keep the focus on the particular individual you are meeting with at the time.

Action Planner

Make the decision to address any performance problems in your workgroup that might not have been addressed in the past. Make sure that you have specific examples to support the feedback you will present to this employee, expecting that there will be denial or resistance to the feedback.

— 3 —
Motivating Top Performers

Think about what it is like providing performance feedback to your top performing employees. At first, you might think that this group would be the easiest to provide feedback for, being top performers. It should be nothing but good news, right? Well, it isn't always that simple, as this chapter will explain.

To begin with, top performers might not always be that easy to identify or differentiate from middle performers. They are usually the highest potential people who work for you. They typically receive the top performance ratings, raises, and other performance bonuses that exist in your organization. They almost always exceed the requirements of the job. They are your best contributors and probably get the most done in the organization. This is the pool of candidates that everyone in the organization wants to go to when looking for someone to fill an internal promotion.

Although it might seem that managing top performers would also be easy, this is not always the case. Keeping an employee who is at this performance level motivated can be a challenge. You can also face perceived "fairness issues," as the top performers might feel they are being asked to do more than others performing at a lower level and they might believe that they are being taken advantage of because they get things done. Providing the right amount of recognition and rewards for your top performers to keep them motivated while they are performing at lower but acceptable levels is something you need to manage. You always run the risk of alienating your other employees by paying too much positive attention to your top performers.

Yesterday's Accomplishments Often Become Today's Performance Standards

What do you think this means with regard to your top performers? It means that probably more and more is being expected, as performance standards for this group often tend to get higher and higher. The standard or performance bar is constantly being raised whenever exceptional performance is achieved, and this then becomes the expectation or standard in the future.

Raising performance standards might keep top performing employees motivated and challenged in their current assignment, which is a good thing. But do you risk setting standards so high that even your top performers can no longer reach this level of performance? If this were to happen, what impact would it have on this group? You run the risk of demotivating even this level of performer. Setting performance standards can be a delicate balance, one that needs to be faced every day when supervising top performers.

Managing Fairness and Equity at Work

Supervisors and managers need to appreciate the innate need for fairness felt by all employees. Nearly everyone has felt at one time or another that he or she wasn't being treated fairly at work, and this is natural and expected for the most part. But work-related fairness issues need to be addressed or at least acknowledged when they get to the point of significantly affecting an employee's job performance, especially with top performers. Listening carefully to how your top performers feel about these types of issues is important to building and maintaining a positive working relationship with them.

You should try to understand whether or not the reward for good performance is perceived as fair and equitable to the employee, and why. For example, what if the reward for doing a good job meant more work? This might sound at first like an unusual way to reinforce great performance, but it is done all the time. The best performing employees are typically given more challenging and difficult assignments. This may or may not be motivating, depending on the employee as well as the nature of the extra work. In some cases, the employee might feel that the extra work will help them reach their career goals and objectives, and thus would perceive this extra work as a reward. In other cases, the employee might feel that doing a good job means being given more work to do without perceiving a reward associated with that extra work. The employee might feel taken advantage of when others are able to get away with doing less work without any consequence to them. Remember that *one employee's reward could be another employee's punishment.*

Inequities felt by employees may be real or perceived on the part of the employee. Regardless, it is important to at least listen to and, if appropriate, address these feelings. Not addressing this issue tends to make the negative feelings grow stronger. Sometimes just listening to how a person feels and acknowledging your understanding of these feelings is all that is needed. Other times, you might need to investigate and determine if the feelings are justified and take appropriate corrective action.

As a supervisor or manager, it is important that you understand how employees feel about being rewarded for all the extra effort they put into their jobs, as illustrated in the following situation:

Sam worked for his employer for over 25 years and was the top performer in the department. He learned how to perform almost every function of the operation during his tenure and was considered the expert on most aspects of the department. He was the "go-to guy" when nobody else knew the answer. Over the years, he trained almost all of the other employees on how to perform their jobs as they were hired into the organization. He still served as a mentor for many of them, sharing the knowledge he had acquired during his long and successful career about how they could perform at higher levels. He had been instrumental in developing procedures for most of the other jobs and even asked to help reorganize the department to make the organization more efficient. Sam was often recognized for his skills and knowledge and was appreciated by everyone who worked with him.

The only difficulty was in finding ways to continuously adequately recognize Sam's contributions. Due to the nature of the business, all of the promotional opportunities above Sam's position level required more education than he had or could realistically expect to ever complete. This left Sam essentially stuck at his level in the organization with no promotional opportunities to aspire to in the future. Over the years, Sam's supervisor had already given him all of the additional responsibilities that he reasonably could.

Making the situation even more challenging was the design of the organization's performance management process. The amount of annual raises was determined by the performance rating that employees received each year. Top performers received the highest raises, middle performers the next highest, and poor performers received no raise or a very low raise. As you would expect, Sam always received the highest raise in the department each year. The problem was that the percentage increase difference between a top performer and a middle performer wasn't very much, maybe a percentage point or two of the employee's base salary. This didn't amount to enough money to serve as any real incentive to those employees like Sam, who really put forth that extra effort to ensure that they not only meet the requirements of their positions, but significantly exceed them as well.

If you find yourself in this predicament, it is important that you continue to try to find ways other than money to reward and recognize your top performers. Sometimes, you might need to be creative in your thinking about what specifically would be most rewarding to the employee. Although everyone would like to make more money for performing their jobs, there are also intangible rewards that can be motivating and rewarding, such as additional responsibilities, special assignments, mentoring other employees, recognition, etc. You need to discover what is most rewarding for each of your employees.

Understanding what is important and motivating for each of your top performers will help you avoid this "rewards gone wrong" scenario. This is why it is extremely important to create a good dialog with your top performers, keeping in tune with their career goals and interests. Simply asking these employees about their career goals and interests and what motivates them can help you provide them with enriching experiences that will be consistent with their job expectations as well as rewarding to them.

Helping Top Performers Succeed

To help top performers succeed, you need to focus on their development in both their current job as well as future assignments. You need to pay attention to their growth, providing them with appropriate career opportunities and giving them greater levels of responsibility based on their current development on the job, as well as be focused and supportive of their future career growth and aspirations. Top performers are usually very strategic in their career strategy and expect you to be as well. They want to feel that what they are currently doing will help them reach their future goals.

Contrary to popular belief, top performers don't automatically get recognized by the organization or get offered opportunities to grow and develop in their careers. This is why there are programs in place to identify high-potential employees and provide them with the experiences and opportunities they need to grow and develop. Top performers need to receive recognition and reinforcement to continue to perform at this level. They may not always be self-motivated, or continue to perform at higher levels, without their supervisors or managers being involved. While it is true that they generally know how to perform their jobs, learn new tasks quickly, and have an interest in learning new skills, they still need your guidance, support, and direction to reach these goals and aspirations. Typically, top performers don't want to be left alone as they perform their jobs. Even though they might not need the same amount of guidance and direction as other employees, they still need attention and guidance at times, especially if they have high aspirations for advancement.

Top performers often pay more attention to other factors in the organization that can affect their careers. They understand how important it is to make a good impression to those in decision-making positions and seek opportunities to be visible to this group. Top performers are typically well-networked. They understand the importance and benefit of staying connected with those they meet during their careers and how to utilize these contacts. Top performers may have a tendency to ignore the chain-of-command of the organization and go directly to the decision makers. In other words, they might want to go around their direct supervisor entirely (going directly to their supervisor's boss) or higher. Top performers often expect to be given access to decision makers, which may or may not be something you will be happy about. You need to understand that this expectation could exist, and deal with these situations in a positive manner to support these employees.

Motivating top performers to continuously achieve higher performance levels is a challenge to you as a supervisor and one that you must accept. You need to understand what motivates your top performers and ensure they are being challenged in the right way and pointed in the right direction. The key is in establishing a dialog between you and your top performers to better understand the particular motivational factors that are most important to them. A performance feedback evaluation meeting can provide the opportunity to begin this discussion, as illustrated in the following case study about a supervisor and one of his most talented employees. In this meeting, the issue of promotional opportunities surfaces as one of the most important keys to motivating the employee. Think about how the supervisor addresses this subject and if you might have approached the situation differently.

CASE STUDY: TOP PERFORMER

Today, a supervisor is going to meet with an employee named Jackie Black who has been one of the best performing employees in the department since joining the company a few years ago. The supervisor has learned that he can always depend on Jackie to do more than is requested and Jackie works hard to make sure that all of the specifics of any task are completed correctly. Jackie always comes to work on time and has missed almost no work since being hired. Jackie, for the most part, interacts well with coworkers and helps others as requested or needed. Jackie always has a positive attitude about the job and is supportive of new initiatives as they are introduced into the workplace. The supervisor plans on rating Jackie as "exceeds requirements" or "exceptional" in most of the performance areas on the evaluation form.

The only real concern that the supervisor has is that this job might not be challenging enough, considering Jackie's talent and potential. Although the supervisor would hate to lose Jackie, at the same time he knows the potential that exists for Jackie to perform at a higher-level position. They have had some discussions about this in the past but have never really addressed the issue specifically. During the performance review today, the supervisor plans on addressing this subject and discussing Jackie's longer-term career interests. However, he is concerned that there might be limited opportunities for advancement for Jackie within the company at the present time.

The supervisor is going to present Jackie with the following completed Performance Evaluation document during this meeting.

Performance Evaluation

Employee's Name: Jackie Black

Position: Customer Service Representative

Date of Evaluation: January 15, 20____

Ratings:

- **Unacceptable:** This is a level of performance that is unacceptable and should not be allowed to continue. Immediate action is needed to address this problem performance.

- **Needs Improvement:** This level of performance needs to be improved and should not be allowed to continue in the future. A plan should be put in place to improve this level of performance to an acceptable level.

- **Meets Requirements:** This is a fully acceptable level of performance. Employees can continue at this performance level throughout their careers.

- **Exceeds Requirements:** This performance level goes beyond what is expected and exceeds the requirements of the job.

- **Exceptional:** This performance level is clearly at the highest level, going well beyond what is required or expected.

SAFETY: Performs the job safely at all times, complies with all safety requirements, wears all protective safety equipment required for the position, follows proper safe work procedures.

Safety Rating:

- ☐ Unacceptable
- ☐ Needs Improvement
- ☐ Meets Requirements
- ☒ Exceeds Requirements
- ☐ Exceptional

Comments: Jackie consistently meets or exceeds the safety requirements of the job. Jackie has led several safety initiatives and teams during the past year and has written safety procedures for the department.

QUALITY: Performs job in a quality manner, follows all required procedures, meets standards at all times, checks quality frequently, understands quality specifications and requirements of each task performed.

Quality Rating:

- ☐ Unacceptable
- ☐ Needs Improvement
- ☐ Meets Requirements
- ☐ Exceeds Requirements
- ☒ Exceptional

Comments: During the past year, Jackie identified a new product quality problem that had previously gone unnoticed. This potentially saved the company a great deal of money, not to mention problems for the customer had this quality problem not been corrected. Jackie received a Quality Commitment Award for this effort.

PRODUCTIVITY: Meets productivity goals, keeps pace with work, overcomes obstacles to efficient operations, seeks ways to increase productivity, minimizes down time, and proactively prevents slowdowns to customer service.

Productivity Rating:

- ☐ Unacceptable
- ☐ Needs Improvement
- ☐ Meets Requirements
- ☒ Exceeds Requirements
- ☐ Exceptional

Comments: Jackie meets or exceeds most of the productivity measures on the job. Jackie has made several suggestions that reduced service delays and improved overall speeds of the service process.

COMMUNICATION: Shares ideas and feelings with others in a positive manner, is open to suggestions and constructive feedback, provides constructive feedback to others, is able to communicate effectively with different levels of employees in the organization, is willing to express him- or herself in front of others, including during meetings.

Communications Rating:

- ☐ Unacceptable
- ☐ Needs Improvement
- ☒ Meets Requirements
- ☐ Exceeds Requirements
- ☐ Exceptional

Comments: Jackie usually is willing to share her ideas with others. Jackie sometimes is less receptive to constructive criticism and should try to keep more of an open mind toward this type of feedback when received from others.

TEAMWORK: Works well with others, assists others in performing their jobs, is willing to help others deal with problems interfering with productivity, deals with conflict in a positive manner, works toward the goals of the team.

Teamwork Rating:

- ☐ Unacceptable
- ☐ Needs Improvement
- ☐ Meets Requirements
- ☒ Exceeds Requirements
- ☐ Exceptional

Comments: Jackie is a team player, but prefers to be in a lead role when working with others. Jackie needs to learn at times to be an equal member of peer groups and make contributions as a member of the team.

RELIABILITY: Regularly comes to work on time, can be depended upon to consistently perform at an acceptable or better level, consistently produces quality work, responds in a consistent and positive manner in all situations, has positive interactions with others on a regular basis.

Reliability Rating:

- ☐ Unacceptable
- ☐ Needs Improvement
- ☐ Meets Requirements
- ☒ Exceeds Requirements
- ☐ Exceptional

Comments: Jackie is a reliable employee in every aspect of the job. Jackie is always early for work and meets every deadline or schedule that must be met. Jackie has a positive, "can-do" attitude concerning every challenge presented to her.

COOPERATION: Contributes ideas to improve workplace and process on a regular basis, contributes to the team's overall efforts, makes an effort to ensure that requirements are met, especially those that directly impact the customer, consistently makes positive contributions to the team. Works positively with everyone on the team. Is willing to do what others ask and provide assistance when needed. Supports the goals and objectives of the team and the entire organization.

Cooperation Rating:

- ☐ Unacceptable
- ☐ Needs Improvement
- ☒ Meets Requirements
- ☐ Exceeds Requirements
- ☐ Exceptional

Comments: Jackie works well with others and cooperates in reaching team goals. Jackie is always willing to do what is asked and usually more.

OVERALL PERFORMANCE RATING COMMENTS:

Jackie is definitely one of the top performers in our workgroup. Jackie has made significant contributions not only to our team, but has also suggested and implemented process improvements to the entire operation. Jackie generally works well with all levels of the organization. She is interested in career advancement and I would like for this to be a priority goal, continuing to seek these types of appropriate opportunities for Jackie during the upcoming performance cycle year.

The following is a discussion between the Supervisor and Jackie during their most recent annual performance feedback session.

Supervisor: Hello Jackie. Today I would like to review your performance for the past year and give you feedback on your career goals with our company.

Jackie: That sounds great. I'm especially interested in talking about any career opportunities that might exist in the company.

Supervisor: I understand. But before we get to that, I would like to review your performance during the past year. I completed this Performance Evaluation form that I would like you to review and sign after we have completed the review today.

Jackie: Okay.

(Supervisor gives Jackie time to review the performance evaluation document)

Supervisor: Jackie, do you have any questions concerning this evaluation?

Jackie: Well, I am concerned about the comment regarding Teamwork—that I need to accept being just a member of a team and not the leader, and only receiving a "Meets Requirements" for Communications. I don't think that is accurate, and it makes it look like I am uncooperative and a poor communicator. I'm worried that this could look bad for me, especially if I'm being considered for a promotion and the hiring manager sees this.

Supervisor: I'm sorry you feel that way. That was not my intention. Overall, this is a very good evaluation; in fact, one of the best in our workgroup. But I feel that I need to give you balanced feedback on your overall performance in order to help you continue to grow and develop in the future. I don't think that these comments should be a problem for you if a prospective hiring manager sees them. However, it could be something that you might be asked about during an interview and you should be prepared to respond. We'll discuss these ratings in more detail later on in this review.

Jackie: Okay.

Supervisor: Let's talk more specifically about the evaluations. I want you to better understand how I decided on these ratings and provide you with more feedback on each of them. Sound okay?

Jackie: Yes.

Supervisor: Let's start with Safety. I rated you as "Exceeds Requirements." As I mentioned in my comments, you have led several safety initiatives including safety teams and you have also written a number of safety procedures for our department. As you know, the nature of our business requires certain safety precautions and instructions for our customers, so this is important to us and I appreciate your extra efforts in this area.

Jackie: I appreciate your comments. I know how important safety is to our function.

Supervisor: Okay, let's move on to Quality. I rated you as "Exceptional" in this area. I believe that your dedication to ensuring that the job gets done correctly is one of your greatest strengths. You are also excellent in spotting quality problems, such as the one that you recently identified before the product was released into the marketplace. You certainly deserved the quality award you received.

Jackie: I do feel that this is one of our most important responsibilities to our customers. After all, that is what we are here to do—serve the customer.

Supervisor: Next, let's look at Productivity. This is another area in which I rated you as "Exceeds Requirements." You made a number of suggestions that made a significant impact on the timeliness of our service, and even helped implement most of them. You set high production standards for yourself and work hard to meet them.

Jackie: Yes, I do have high standards that I hold myself and others to when it comes to meeting the demands of this job. I am a little disappointed that you didn't rate me as exceptional in this area considering the things you mentioned.

Supervisor: Okay, I understand. But this rating doesn't diminish what you have accomplished in this area. Again, an "Exceeds Requirements" rating is a very good rating and I do think that you could reach the Exceptional level if you continue to perform at this level of productivity in the future.

Jackie: Again, I appreciate this and will continue to work hard in this area and hopefully earn a higher evaluation next year. I always strive to be as productive as I can in everything I do.

Supervisor: Let's talk about the next area—Communications. I know you were disappointed by both the rating I gave you and the comments concerning your performance in this area. I think we should spend some extra time with this. I want to make sure you leave this discussion with specific feedback about how you can improve your performance in this area in the future. I observed a couple of things about you concerning communications that I think are important enough for you to be made aware of. You are usually willing to share your ideas and thoughts about how we can improve our customer service, but there are times when it seems that you are holding back your thoughts or even feelings about a decision that has been made by someone else. I am not sure why this is the case. Is it that you don't like the idea, or that you think it isn't the appropriate way to go, or what?

Jackie: Well, that's mostly the reason. Sometimes I feel that others in our group get tired of hearing my ideas and want to express some of their own. I even feel that there could be some resentment on their part. I overheard some comments indicating that "I think I know it all" or something like that. I just don't want to appear as if I only like my own suggestions or ideas. I don't exactly know how to deal with this sometimes.

Supervisor: I appreciate your candor in sharing how you feel about this. I'm afraid that the way you are approaching this might be making it worse. When you don't weigh in on other people's ideas or suggestions, it makes it seem that you don't agree which, based on what you are telling me, isn't necessarily always the case. Right?

Jackie: Yes, that is absolutely correct. A lot of times I do agree and think that there have been some excellent suggestions, often much better than mine. A number of the other CSR's have been doing this job for a lot longer than me and have all that experience going for them.

Supervisor: Then you should tell them that. Don't be silent about your ideas. Many times, it's the discussions we have that develop the ideas that get us to the best decisions. We need you in these discussions!

Jackie: Okay, I'll give this some thought and find a way to be more involved in discussions.

Supervisor: Great. The other thing I wanted to talk to you about in this area has to do with how you have been responding to constructive criticism of any kind. I have seen a number of occasions that when someone gives you this type of feedback, you are less than receptive and sometimes get defensive. I have had several others comment on this and they feel reluctant to even bring up anything to you that might challenge your ideas. That isn't consistent with the way we all work together in our group. We don't give each other this type of feedback to be mean or to hurt feelings, but rather to try to help each of us to do a better job in the future. This can be the most valuable feedback you ever receive, but you are cutting yourself off from this dialog with others because of the way you react to it.

Jackie: I'm not sure I understand. Can you give me an example?

Supervisor: Yes. Just last week, John offered you a suggestion on one of the specifications you wrote on that new product when you showed these specs to the group during our Monday meeting. You told John that you didn't agree with him; in fact, you told him that his suggestion was wrong and a bad idea. My sense was that John was hurt by the way you handled the situation. John has had many years of experience and his suggestion deserved to be considered based on its merits. Just being right isn't enough when dealing with others if it causes damage to your working relations with them. You need to respect other people's ideas and understand that they put a lot of themselves into these ideas.

Jackie: I guess I see your point. I like and respect John and I didn't mean to offend him. Should I talk to him about this?

Supervisor: That's a decision you need to make for yourself, but I would say it might be a good idea. The point that I want you to understand is that you need to be more open to others' opinions and ideas, giving them a chance to be fully understood and have their ideas discussed without getting defensive if those ideas are different from yours.

Jackie: Okay, I'll try to work on this.

Supervisor: The next thing I would like to discuss is Teamwork. You said earlier that you were also concerned about the comment I made concerning this area.

Jackie: I always have considered myself to be a great team player and you even told me so in the past. I don't understand why you made this negative comment about my teamwork skills.

Supervisor: Again, I did rate you as "Exceeds Requirements" in this area and said that you are a good team player. I meant it or I wouldn't have written it on your evaluation. What I have observed is that you prefer to be the leader of any work teams we establish and if you are not, you tend to retreat a little bit when it comes to team participation. I notice that in these circumstances, you get less involved in both the group discussions and in implementing the follow-up action items. My sense in this case is that you feel that if it isn't your team to lead, then you are less interested in participating. You need to understand that learning to become a good leader starts with being a good follower as well. As we have discussed, there are a number of other very experienced people in the group who also want a chance to play a leadership role from time to time, and they deserve to be given these opportunities as well.

Jackie: I do see what you mean. Thanks for the feedback. I'll try to deal with this differently from now on.

Supervisor: Let's move on to Reliability. Again, I gave you a high rating in this area. You are very dependable and work hard to make sure that you meet our demanding schedules. There isn't a challenge that I have given to you that you haven't given 100 percent to not only complete, but also to meeting the deadline for completion. We have all learned to rely on you since you have joined our team.

Jackie: I do work hard to meet all the requirements of the job every day. But again, I'm curious as to why I didn't receive an "Exceptional" rating in this area.

Supervisor: I think that this is also something that would be entirely possible in the future. Exceptional ratings are rare and sometimes require performance to be observed over time. I think reliability is something that falls into this category. Again, this doesn't take away from your performance in this area—not at all. The last performance area is "Cooperation." As you see, I rated you as "Meets Requirements" in this area.

Jackie: I see that and I also wanted to ask you why I wasn't rated higher in this area? You said in your comments that I always do what is asked of me and more! I don't understand.

Supervisor: Well, this goes back to the discussion that we had concerning Communication. The two areas in this case relate to one another. I believe if you improve in one area, it will be reflected in the other.

Jackie: Well, that seems to me to be a bit like double jeopardy and I'm being penalized twice for the same thing!

Supervisor: I don't see it that way. It's just that I can't rate you as higher in Cooperation at this point, based on the things we have previously discussed. But again, I have every confidence that you are going to address this and be able to receive higher ratings in both areas next year. If you don't have any other comments on this area, let's move on to your overall evaluation, which was rated as "Exceeds Requirements." This is a great rating, and you should be proud of your accomplishments since beginning to work for us a relatively short time ago. It's really significant to achieve this level of performance in such a short period of time.

Jackie: Thank you. As you know, I do have very high personal standards and won't be satisfied in the future with anything less than an "Exceptional" rating. I'll continue to strive to reach this goal. I'm very interested in career advancement and was hoping that we could spend some more time discussing these possibilities.

Supervisor: Of course. I was planning on this before we concluded our discussion today. I have discussed your potential and interest in career advancement opportunities with others in the organization, so everyone in decision-making positions is aware of you. The problem is that there don't seem to be any opportunities available that would be appropriate for you at this time. How ever, I'll keep watching for the right opportunities. They will come along. I just don't want to see you get too impatient and start looking outside the company for such an opportunity. We are very impressed with you and would hate to lose you. I have also talked to our Human Resource department about this, and I encourage you to do the same.

Jackie: Well, I am concerned that I might get overlooked for any opportunities that exist now or in the future. I saw that Helen got a promotion just last week that I thought I should have at least been considered for. I guess I should tell you that I did ask to meet with the Director of that area to talk about why I was overlooked for that opportunity. We are meeting next week in his office. I'm the type of person who likes to be in control of their future. I sometimes feel that I would have more control over what jobs I can apply for outside the company than from within. I have become aware of several jobs in the area that are available that would offer me the leadership role I'm seeking, but I like working here and would rather stay with this company.

Supervisor: I'm not going to discuss other people's performance with you, but I will say that Helen did have many years of experience that made her the best qualified person for that particular position. Experience will always be something that is very important to us when we look at candidates for any position. I'm pleased that you do want to stay with our company and believe

	that the right opportunity will come your way. You just have to be patient. Also, I am fine with your going to the Director about your concerns. I know him very well; we've worked together for years now. I might be able to give you some guidance on how to best approach him, and be prepared for this meeting.
Jackie:	Yes, I guess it would be a good idea to meet with you first. I hadn't thought of it. Thanks. I guess patience isn't one of my strongest skills, especially when it comes to my career advancement. I will try to be more patient on this but I can't make any guarantees!
Supervisor:	Okay, I understand. Let me set another time for us to talk before your meeting with the Director next week as we are about out of time now. Before we close, do you have any other questions that we haven't addressed today?
Jackie:	No, I believe you've covered everything.
Supervisor:	Okay, great. I would again like to say that I do see you as a valuable member of our team, and that you have excellent potential for career growth in the future. Thanks for all your hard work and contributions.

Performance Feedback Evaluation Meeting Debrief

Perhaps the biggest challenge this supervisor faced during this discussion were the factors that he had little or no control over, especially concerning the availability of promotional opportunities in the near future for this employee. The supervisor did a good job of being candid and honest with the employee concerning this situation and showed empathy for the employee concerning her feelings about the situation. This is very important to employees, especially top performing employees. The working relationship a supervisor has with his or her employees is a very important factor in determining an employee's overall job satisfaction. Often, employees don't really leave their employers but rather they leave their supervisors when they seek other employment opportunities. This came out during the discussion as the employee expressed the desire to remain employed by the organization, provided that there was at least some visibility for future career growth and opportunities. A supervisor in such a case must be cognizant of both the importance of maintaining a positive working relationship and communication with this employee, but also of keeping focused on her career goals as well.

You might agree that this supervisor actually did a good job in presenting performance feedback to this employee as well as addressing her concerns. There are a number of subtleties that take place in any discussion of this kind, which go back and forth during the dialog. The following questions address many of these subtleties as well as specific issues relating to this employee's situation which involve the true feelings of both the supervisor and the employee.

1. How well do you think this supervisor conducted the performance feedback meeting with Jackie?

2. Did the supervisor do a good job in presenting balanced feedback?

3. Did the supervisor have specific examples to support some of the feedback he presented to the employee? What were some examples? Why do you think this would be important?

4. How well do you think Jackie responded to the constructive criticism presented by the supervisor? Do you think Jackie will change behaviors in the future as a result?

5. Do you think that the employee responded appropriately to all of the feedback received during this evaluation? Was Jackie out of line with some responses or were they appropriate for the situation and circumstances?

6. How well do you think the supervisor handled this employee's questions concerning the rationale for some of his ratings? Did the supervisor get defensive or simply present his rationale for his ratings and comments?

7. Do you feel that this supervisor was holding back on some of the ratings by not giving Jackie a higher or highest rating to give her something to strive for in the future? If so, do you think this was a fair or unfair thing to do? Do you feel that this would be a good strategy for you to follow with your highest performing employees? Why or why not?

8. How well do you think the supervisor addressed Jackie's interest in promotional opportunities?

9. How well do you think this supervisor responded to the news that the employee was going *over his head* concerning career opportunities?

10. Do you think that Jackie will stay with this organization or leave to seek promotional opportunities elsewhere? What do you think would be the best decision for Jackie to make?

11. What would you have done differently if you were the supervisor conducting the performance feedback evaluation meeting?

Chapter Review

1. Do you feel that it is easier or harder to provide performance feedback to top performing employees? Why or why not?

2. Do you agree that yesterday's accomplishments often become today's performance standards? What experiences have you had when this became a reality?

3. Have you ever tried to provide a reward or reinforcement to someone that was actually more of a punishment to that person? How did you learn what the result was from this effort to reward or recognize someone? How could you have done this better?

4. How do you feel if someone who works for you goes over or around you to someone higher up in the organization? What would be the best way to deal with this type of situation?

5. If you are like most people, at one time or another you have felt that you were treated unfairly at any time during your career. How did this feel? How can you use your own experiences feeling this way to help those who report to you deal with their feelings of inequity on their jobs?

Top Performer Feedback Tips

- Talk to your highest-level employees frequently to keep in touch with their feelings about being given more challenging assignments than others. Make sure you address any feelings of inequities they may have concerning these assignments.

- Don't wait until the annual performance feedback meeting to discuss your top performers' career goals and aspirations. During the performance year, frequently discuss these career goals with employees to ensure that they know you support these goals and to make adjustments to their developmental plans, as appropriate.

- Discuss your top performers' career goals with other decision makers in the organization to ensure that they are aware of these goals and provide their support.

- Delegate extensively to top performers in accordance with their experience and skill level, as appropriate. Give them challenging assignments that might not feel appropriate for other levels of performers.

- Encourage top performers to help others perform their jobs more effectively.

- Provide additional training opportunities to top performers. Challenge them to learn things that might not typically be part of their current level or job.

- Assign a mentor to top performers to help them receive the guidance and support that they might need to reach their potential. This will also provide someone outside of their reporting structure to provide a different perspective.

- Top performers do want more of your time than other employees because they want to interact, receive feedback and guidance, and discuss more complex aspects of their jobs and the organization as a whole. Providing this time is a good investment in the development of these individuals.

- Provide "stretch" opportunities to top performers, such as assigning them to an important project or even recommending them for a promotion. "Stretch" opportunities give top performers the challenge they typically seek as well as a chance to prove their abilities.

- Recognize top performers by acknowledging their contributions and celebrate their success along with them. As a supervisor or manager of top performers, you should also feel a sense of accomplishment for their successes, as you play an important role in providing them with these opportunities.

Action Planner

Set up more frequent meetings with top performers to keep updated on their career goals and provide them with regular feedback on their progress toward these goals.

— 4 —
Managing Middle Performers

M iddle performers are those employees that are typically considered as successful on the job but that do not perform at the same higher level as top performers. However, middle performers do contribute significantly to any organization and perform important jobs making great contributions to the company. There is nothing wrong with being a middle-level performer, as they are performing at an acceptable level and should be able to perform at this level throughout their careers. They are also a very important segment of your employee population, particularly as the majority of employees in any organization will fall into this group. If you look at the overall performance level of employees in an organization, you will typically find that about 70 percent of employees would be considered middle performers or by a description, that would be appropriate for this level of performance. Based on this statistic, another way of describing this group would be to say that they are the average performers in the organization.

However, most middle performers would not be content being considered an average performer and would probably take offense being described as such. They often have higher career aspirations which at some point in their career can become a major point of frustration for them. However, despite these frustrations, many middle performers do more than just punch the clock or do the minimum requirements of their job. At times, they excel well above the average performance level and need to be recognized when they do. The jobs performed by middle-level performers are often very complex and would be challenging to any employee, including top performers. The difference often lies in the potential that employees have to move to levels beyond their present position in the organization.

Middle performers are sometimes difficult to identify and distinguish from top performers. Again, this is true because often they might perform at levels closer to that of top performers or at times even perform at higher levels. They might have been considered a top performer at one time in their careers. They also often perceive themselves as either being top performers or as aspiring to become top performers.

Measuring middle performers can be difficult because the performance indicators may not accurately reflect an individual's contributions or effort. These indicators usually show that the employee performed the duties expected, but might not reflect the importance or actual value of such duties. Middle performers are often involved in many activities on their jobs, either by assignment or by their own choosing. This can sometimes result in high activity, but with no clear focus on results. There is a distinction between high activity and achieving desired results. This is something that can be confusing to many middle performers who may feel that they should be rated higher, at least in part, because of how busy they are on their jobs. As a supervisor or manager, you need to be careful not to confuse activity with achievement. Remember that there is a distinction between doing the *right things* versus *doing things right.*

Employees will often cite all of their activities as accomplishments at the end of the year to make their case for being evaluated at a higher level. Sometimes this occurs because employees tend to gravitate toward those duties or responsibilities of their job that they enjoy the most. Employees might excel in performing their favorite duties and focus as much of their time as they can on these duties. It is fine to allow employees to pursue those aspects of their jobs that they most enjoy, but not at the exclusion of other more important responsibilities of their jobs. This is also fine as long as these activities add value to their job. However, employees shouldn't be permitted to choose their own responsibilities if they are not in alignment with the goals of the organization. They key is in establishing and communicating the goals that middle performers should be working towards, and these goals be in alignment with the rest of the organization, as illustrated below:

If these goals are not in alignment, then there is far less likelihood that an employee can be a successfully contributing member of the organization. This is why it is so important for a manager or supervisor to ensure that employees are working on the right things, and that they are aligned with the organization's overall goals. Ideally, the goals of employees as well as the organization can be achieved through this goal alignment.

Setting expectations and measuring performance against goals and expectations is the best way to keep employees focused on the right things.

On the flip side, sometimes employees might avoid certain duties, especially those that they don't like to perform. However, these duties may be critical to the performance of the job and the needs of the organization. Employees should not be allowed to skip certain duties, especially if they are critical. However, as a manager or supervisor, you need to give employees guidance and direction concerning how they invest their time and the company's resources and whether these efforts are in alignment with their organizational goals and objectives. It is often very helpful to seek feedback from others concerning a middle performer's contributions to gain the perspectives of others on their contributions to the goals of the organization.

Today, many employees are supervised from a distance. This makes it especially difficult to supervise middle performers because you are not able to evaluate their day-to-day activities. Also, when a manager or supervisor has many direct reports, it is even more challenging to assess middle performers accurately.

The Importance of Establishing Effective Supervisory Communications

You don't have to be the best communicator in the world to communicate effectively with your employees. What is most important is that you communicate with your employees in a manner and style most comfortable and effective for you. In other words, just be yourself. Take the time to communicate with your employees on a regular basis on topics that are of interest and beneficial to them in their job performance.

It is important to establish two-way communication with those who report to you. Employees should feel that, based on job experience and expertise, they have something important to say and that others, especially you as their supervisor, will listen to them. You can learn a great deal communicating with those who report to you, especially if there is a two-way exchange of information. Really listening to what your employees are saying can be the key to helping them become more engaged. They will share this information with you, but you have to listen to what they are saying. Communicating candidly and honestly with your direct reports helps build leadership credibility and trust.

When communicating, don't always assume that you are being understood. As a supervisor or manager, it is important to stay in the communication long enough to make sure that you are understood, and that you understand others.

There is a story about a supervisor named Leon who had been in his job for over 30 years. He was one of the most respected supervisors in the company, in part because he was such a good communicator. Leon wasn't a great public speaker, never had any formal communications training, and didn't typically go around making profound statements. But everyone always left any discussion with him with a clear understanding of what he expected of them.

Here is what Leon did to achieve this level of communication: Every time Leon gave instructions to one of his employees, he asked that person to repeat the instructions back to him. His employees quickly learned that they needed to pay very close attention to everything Leon said because he would test them on their understanding of the assignment. After receiving his instructions, employees would often ask him for clarification on the assignment. Leon always had the full attention of his employees every time he communicated with them. Just saying that you understood wasn't good enough for Leon—you had to demonstrate your understanding. Leon even repeated this process with others who didn't report to him. He would ask people on all levels of the organization what they agreed upon during their conversation before concluding the interaction. In this way, Leon made everyone he had contact with a better listener when talking with him.

Communications Makes a Difference

Communication often determines the success or failure of the middle stars. Do your middle performers know what great performance looks like and what is really expected of them? They might never have been told what is required to become a top performer. This may require you to be able to describe what behaviors you expect from employees in specific terms. It is important to provide them with guidance that can help them better understand what is considered to be great or top performance and what they would need in order to do to reach this performance level. Providing specific examples is important in order to demonstrate exactly what performance you are expecting. Describe exactly the behaviors you expect that would make a significant difference in the individual's performance, such as spending extra time on a project or describing what is considered to be an example of providing especially good customer service.

For example, if a Customer Service Representative is not serving customers in the most desirable manner, his or her supervisor needs to describe, in specific terms, what are the desired behaviors to improve his or her performance (for example, following up on orders to ensure that the customer was fully satisfied). Building confidence by reinforcing desirable behaviors, even if in incremental steps, can help employees achieve those desired performance levels. The key is to ensure that middle performers clearly understand what is expected of them and that they receive feedback on how well they are meeting the requirements of their positions.

Sometimes, a supervisor and an employee have different perceptions of what is important in the performance of a job, as illustrated below. This often results in performance expectations not being met.

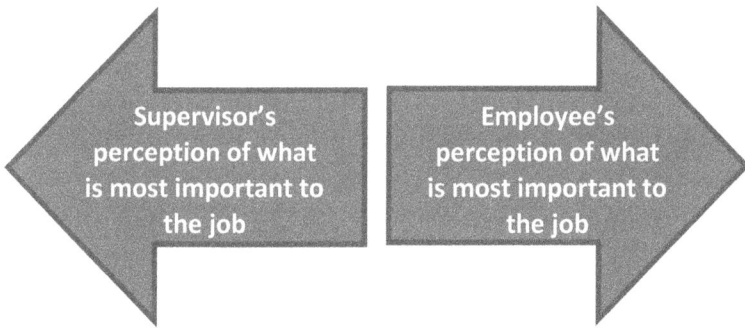

Supervisor's perception of what is most important to the job

Employee's perception of what is most important to the job

As can be seen, the supervisor and employee have very different perceptions about what is most important in performing the job. This type of disconnect can cause many issues between the supervisor and employee, including how the employee may ultimately be evaluated by the supervisor. The supervisor expects one set of deliverables, while the employee is focused on other factors he or she might believe to be most important.

Unfortunately, the employee might be doing an excellent job performing those aspects of the job less important to the supervisor.

This situation must be reversed, as illustrated:

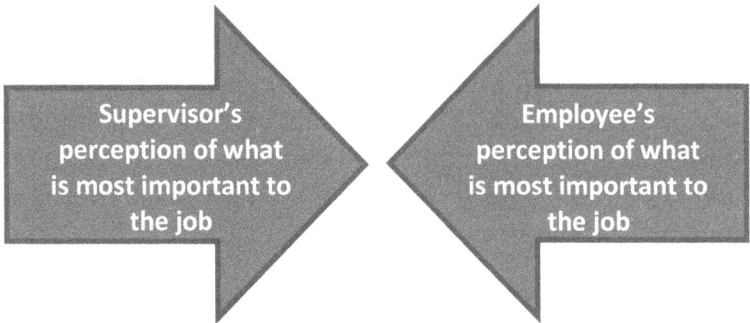

| Supervisor's perception of what is most important to the job | Employee's perception of what is most important to the job |

There must be a clear dialog between supervisor and employee concerning what is most important on a job. The ultimate responsibility for ensuring that misunderstandings do not occur lies with the supervisor.

The interesting thing is that often, these differences might not be readily apparent to the supervisor and employee, or at least not acknowledged if known. These perceptions must be shared between supervisor and employee to ensure that they are on the same page concerning what is most important.

While perceptions should be addressed, what is most important should not always be solely determined by the supervisor, except in cases when the employee is new to the job. Differing perceptions can become a constant source of frustration if not addressed, and could be the reason that middle performers do not receive higher evaluations. More effective communication between employees and supervisors can help prevent this from happening in the future.

Coaching employees on a daily or regular basis can make a big difference between the success and failure of middle stars. Spending time with middle performers can pay great dividends and help these employees contribute at higher levels. The fact that middle performers comprise the greatest percentage of the workforce makes their contributions even more important. What contributes to the performance of these middle employees can vary tremendously. However, the key to managing or supervising these employees is to ensure that they clearly understand what is expected of them and that they receive feedback on how well they meet the requirements of their positions. Middle performers are challenging to supervisors, often because this group is not satisfied with being told that they are middle performers. It is important to provide them with guidance that can help them better understand what would be considered great or top performance and what they need to do to reach this performance level.

It is important to acknowledge the accomplishments of middle performers, particularly those who rise to the next performance level. It is also important to provide middle performers with timely and frequent specific feedback on what they are doing that is in alignment with organizational goals (which you want to see continue) as well as those activities that might not be in alignment with these goals, to keep them focused on the right things.

Create incentives for middle performers to continue to grow on their job, as it is important for these employees to feel that you are interested in their career development. This is the part of the performance feedback that employees are typically most interested in receiving. Be accessible to middle performers to discuss their career and personal development. As a manager or supervisor, you will find this to be a very good investment of your time.

Reward positive performance by providing middle performers with increased responsibility or more important tasks or assignments to help build their skills and confidence. Provide developmental opportunities for middle performers, including mentoring with higher-level performers, to help them grow and develop as they need this support. During performance feedback meetings, do not skip over the career development part of the discussion, as this is almost always very important.

Let's take a look at the following case study involving a middle performer:

CASE STUDY: MIDDLE PERFORMER

Gene Adams has worked for the company for over 20 years. Over these years, Gene has performed most of the functions of the organization and is knowledgeable about how the various processes interrelate to one another. Gene is considered to be a good employee who does what he is expected to do in performing his job. He is generally reliable, but does need to be reminded about attendance from time to time. Recently, this has been a problem, and his supervisor is planning on discussing this during their performance evaluation later on in the day.

During the performance evaluation, Gene's supervisor plans on encouraging Gene to become more involved in some of the employee engagement initiatives being introduced as a result of a recent engagement survey conducted at the organization.

The supervisor feels that Gene has much more to contribute than he presently does, based on his experience and knowledge of the entire operation. It is hard to predict

---

how Gene will respond to encouragement to become more involved in these types of activities, as he has shown little interest in the past in doing more than what he has been asked to do. The supervisor is going to present Gene with the following completed performance evaluation document during this meeting.

Performance Evaluation

Employee's Name: Gene Adams

Position: Service Representative

Date of Evaluation: December 20, 20____

Ratings:

- **Unacceptable:** This is a level of performance that is unacceptable and should not be allowed to continue. Immediate action is needed to address this problem performance.

- **Needs Improvement:** This level of performance needs to be improved and should not be allowed to continue in the future. A plan should be put in place to improve this level of performance to an acceptable level.

- **Meets Requirements:** This is a fully acceptable level of performance. Employees can continue at this performance level throughout their careers.

- **Exceeds Requirements:** This performance level goes beyond what is expected and exceeds the requirements of the job.

- **Exceptional:** This performance level is clearly at the highest level, going well beyond what is required or expected.

SAFETY: Performs the job safely at all times, complies with all safety requirements, wears all protective safety equipment required for the position, follows proper safe work procedures.

Safety Rating:

- ☐ Unacceptable
- ☐ Needs Improvement
- ☒ Meets Requirements
- ☐ Exceeds Requirements
- ☐ Exceptional

Comments: Gene consistently wears all of his safety equipment and follows all safety rules.

QUALITY: Performs job in a quality manner, follows all required procedures, meets standards at all times, checks quality frequently, understands quality specifications and requirements of each task performed.

Quality Rating:

- ☐ Unacceptable
- ☐ Needs Improvement
- ☒ Meets Requirements
- ☐ Exceeds Requirements
- ☐ Exceptional

Comments: Gene generally performs his job in a quality manner, following the standard operating procedures for all of the tasks of his position.

PRODUCTIVITY: Meets productivity goals, keeps pace with work, overcomes obstacles to efficient operations, seeks ways to increase productivity, minimizes downtime, and proactively prevents slowdowns to process interruptions.

Quality Rating:

- ☐ Unacceptable
- ☐ Needs Improvement
- ☒ Meets Requirements
- ☐ Exceeds Requirements
- ☐ Exceptional

Comments: Gene meets the productivity and standards of the operation, but at times could be more proactive in preventing service delays by better anticipating problems before they occur.

COMMUNICATIONS: Shares ideas and feelings with others in a positive manner, is open to suggestions and constructive feedback, provides constructive feedback to others, is able to communicate effectively with different levels of employees in the organization, is willing to express him- or herself in front of others, including during meetings.

Communications Rating:

- ☐ Unacceptable
- ☐ Needs Improvement
- ☒ Meets Requirements
- ☐ Exceeds Requirements
- ☐ Exceptional

Comments: Although rated as "Meets Requirements" on this performance factor, Gene at times finds himself in conflict with certain employees in our workgroup. Some of these employees have even expressed the desire to be assigned to other areas to avoid working around Gene. However, this is not a problem with others who Gene has been friends with over the years.

TEAMWORK: Works well with others, assists others in performing their jobs, is willing to help others deal with problems interfering with productivity, deals with conflict in a positive manner, works toward the goals of the team.

Communications Rating:

- ☐ Unacceptable
- ☐ Needs Improvement
- ☒ Meets Requirements
- ☐ Exceeds Requirements
- ☐ Exceptional

Comments: I would like to see Gene work to maintain positive working relationships with all of the members of our workgroup going forward.

RELIABILITY: Regularly comes to work on time, can be depended upon to consistently perform at an acceptable or better level, consistently produces quality work, responds in a consistent and positive manner in all situations, has positive interactions with others on a regular basis.

Reliability Rating:

- ☐ Unacceptable
- ☒ Needs Improvement
- ☐ Meets Requirements
- ☐ Exceeds Requirements
- ☐ Exceptional

Comments: Gene is beginning to have an absentee problem and has missed more days than the departmental average. I would like to see Gene improve his attendance in the future to avoid any further actions that might result.

COOPERATION: Contributes ideas to improve workplace and process on a regular basis, contributes to the team's overall efforts, makes an effort to ensure that requirements are met, especially those that directly impact the customer, consistently makes positive contributions to the team. Works positively with everyone on the team. Is willing to do what others ask and provide assistance when needed. Supports the goals and objectives of the team and the entire organization.

Cooperation Rating:

- ☐ Unacceptable
- ☐ Needs Improvement
- ☐ Meets Requirements
- ☒ Exceeds Requirements
- ☐ Exceptional

Comments: Gene is cooperative and provides good ideas on how to better serve the customer. He always does what is asked and required of the position.

OVERALL PERFORMANCE RATING COMMENTS:

Overall, Gene has done a good job over the past year. The only areas of improvement I would like to see during the next year are for Gene to improve his working relationships with certain employees in our workgroup, and lower his level of absenteeism.

The following is the discussion between the Supervisor and Gene during their most recent annual performance feedback session.

Supervisor: Good morning, Gene. It's time to sit down and discuss your performance during the past year. How do you think things have been going for you?

Gene: I haven't had any problems. Everything seems to be going good as far as I know. Unless you are going to tell me something different?

Supervisor: Well, overall, I do agree with you that it has been another good year for you. As in years past, I will cover specifically how I evaluated you on each of the performance areas on the evaluation form. Does that sound okay?

Gene: Yeah, I guess so.

Supervisor: Then let's get started. I have the completed performance evaluation for you to review and will give you a copy after we complete this meeting. So let's go through it now, beginning with the Safety rating. I rated you as "Meets Requirements" in this area. In our business, we only have a few safety rules that need to be followed and you are always in compliance with these. However, I don't want to minimize the importance of following these safety standards and I appreciate your commitment to this area.

Gene: I do believe that it's important to be safe, even in this job. So you don't have to tell me how important it is to follow the rules. I want to go home the same as I came in to work each day.

Supervisor: I certainly have the same goal for everyone each day as well. Let's move on to Quality. I also rated you as "Meets Requirements" in this area. My comment is that *Gene generally performs his job in a quality manner, following the standard operating procedures for all of the tasks of his position.* I think that you do a good job regarding paying attention to the quality standards of your job.

Gene: I am a little concerned that you said I only *generally* perform my job in a quality manner. I think that I consistently pay attention to quality. Can you give me an example of when I don't?

Supervisor: Gene, first, I want to point out that I did rate you as Meeting Requirements in this area. This is a good rating, so I'm not saying that I have a big concern about you. However, there have been a few occasions when I felt that you could have paid more attention in this area. If you remember, there were a few customer complaints that could be tracked back to quality issues that involved service you had provided to those customers. I just wanted to point these out so we can better prevent the same problems from occurring in the future.

Gene: We talked about these complaints at the time they occurred and I thought we concluded that customer was expecting more than our service contract covered. I don't understand why you are now blaming me for those problems.

Supervisor: Gene, please understand that I am not blaming you for those problems and my assessment of what was the root cause of the problems hasn't changed. But the point is that we still had customer complaints and we are all responsible on some level for these complaints. Our job is trying to ensure that we achieve 100 percent customer satisfaction. In this case, it may have been making sure that the customer clearly understood what the service contract covered and didn't cover.

Gene: I still don't feel that I should be blamed for service contracts that I didn't write. Even if we read the service contract to our customers every day, they still will complain that we are not covering enough.

Supervisor: Okay, I do understand how you feel about this. But we have a lot to cover, so let's move on to Productivity if that's alright. Again, I rated you as "Meets Requirements." On this, I said that you do a good job meeting the productivity standards for your job, but I would like to see you be more proactive in anticipating what could cause delays before they actually occur. This is where I think your years of experience can really help us. For example, do you remember when we had a delay in providing service to one of our major customers earlier this year? When we talked about it at the time, you had a number of ideas about how we could have prevented these delays from occurring, but as far as I know, none of these ideas have been put in place. This is why I would like to see you become more proactively involved in the future, and why I made that comment.

Gene: Yes, I do remember when that problem occurred, and I did have some ideas about how we could have prevented these problems, but most of those were the responsibility of other people and not part of my job. I don't really see what I could have done personally to prevent problems from happening.

Supervisor: My point is that you need to share your ideas on how to provide better service to our customers, even if it is outside of your area of responsibility. Based on your experience and knowledge, I believe you can have a positive influence even outside the scope of your job responsibilities. We can talk more at a later time about what you can do to become more involved.

For now, let's move on to Communication. I also rated you as "Meets Requirements" in this area. However, I did comment that you have had a problem with your communications with certain other employees in our group and several have expressed interest in being assigned to an area where they don't have to work with you.

Gene: We both know who you are talking about, and you know as well as I do that this really isn't my fault. Nobody gets along with them. They are always looking for ways to blame others for their mistakes and I am not going to let them get away with that with me. I think that you should be having this talk with them, not me, about how they communicate with their co-workers! As you said in the comments, I get along just fine with everyone else.

Supervisor: Yes, I agree that you do get along with everyone else, but I still would like to see you make more of an effort to work positively with everyone in the workgroup. If you have certain issues with particular people, then you should address them and try to resolve your issues with them. I'm willing to help you do this if you would like me to.

Gene: No, I can handle it myself. I don't want them pulling down my performance ratings.

Supervisor: Okay then, let's move on to Teamwork, where I also rated you as "Meets Requirements." My comment was related to the same problem we just talked about.

Gene: I am really disappointed that I'm getting negative comments in this area for something that, again, I can't do much about. But like I said, I am going to take care of this issue so it won't be a problem in the future.

Supervisor: Okay, but like I said, I'm willing to help you resolve these problems. I just want to make sure that this situation doesn't continue or even get worse. I would suggest that you sit down with these other employees and find a way to work out your differences. But if you insist on handling this yourself, I guess I'll agree to that for now. I'll be paying attention to this situation and might still get involved if I feel it's necessary.

Let's move on. The next area that we need to talk about is Reliability. As you can see, I rated you as Needs Improvement in this area. This was the only factor where I rated you this low. The reason for this rating is based on your absenteeism lately. You have had a good absentee record up to this year. Is there anything that I need to understand that might be contributing to this problem?

Gene: No, there isn't. I really don't understand why I deserve such a low rating for just missing a few more days this year than in the past. I see a lot of others who miss more work than I do every year. Are they being rated as "Needs Improvement" in this area, like I am? I think you should look at my entire work record before coming up with this evaluation. I really don't think this rating is fair!

Supervisor: Well first, I am not going to discuss other people's ratings with you just as I wouldn't discuss yours with them. All I can tell you is that I hold everyone to the same standard. This is an important performance measure in our business because our customers need service every day. When you are not here, they don't always get the kind of service they expect and deserve. I do understand that sometimes we all have to miss work from time to time for any number of reasons that we can't always control. Based on your attendance record over the years, I have every reason to believe that this won't continue to be a problem in the future, but I believe that we should discuss your current absenteeism, and that it should be reflected accurately on your evaluation.

Gene: I'm not really asking you to tell me how you rated others. I just want to make sure that everyone is being treated in the same way, and held to the same standards. I also hope that I don't need to miss as many days next year, so this shouldn't be an issue again, but I really feel this rating is unfair.

Supervisor: I hear you and understand how you feel. If you don't have anything else you want to discuss about this area, I would like to move on to the last area, which is Cooperation.

Gene: Okay.

Supervisor: I rated you as "Exceeds Requirements" in Cooperation. I believe this is your strongest performance area. I feel that you come to work each day wanting to do a good job and do whatever you are asked to do to better serve the customer.

Gene: I'm happy you recognize this. I do work hard to do whatever is asked of me and want to make sure that the job gets done right. I take a lot of pride in my work.

Supervisor: Yes, I agree that you do, and it shows. Finally, let's talk about your overall performance rating. This means that I'm satisfied with your overall performance and think you do a good job servicing our customers, and that I appreciate your contributions to the team.

Gene: Okay, I guess I am good with this rating, although I still think I should be rated higher on most of the things we talked about today.

Supervisor: I believe that you could perform at a higher level in most of these areas than you do today, although as I said, this is a very acceptable performance rating. Are there things that you would like to do or become involved in beyond what you are presently doing? You've been doing this job for a number of years and I have found that experienced employees often need additional challenges to stay motivated on the job.

Gene: I don't know. What would you suggest?

Supervisor: Well, there are a number of work teams that we have initiated lately as part of our employee engagement programs. I don't recall you participating in any of these teams. Many of them are focused on better meeting the requirements of the customer, which is something that I know you are interested in. I don't have all the information on these teams or which ones might be interested in new members with me now, but let me check on this and we can look at those you might be interested in joining. Does that sound okay?

Gene:	I think so. Let me know.
Supervisor:	I will. Let's close now, but before we do this again, I would like to summarize our discussion by saying that I think you are a valuable member of our team and I would like to thank you for all your efforts.

Performance Feedback Evaluation Meeting Debrief

Evaluating middle performers is often a challenge. Many times, as was true in this case, these employees often see themselves performing at a higher level than their supervisors see them performing at. The leadership challenge here is to provide candid and honest feedback to middle performers without demotivating them with regard to all the other positive things they bring to the job. Think about how this supervisor approached these issues and the tone he set for the meeting. You may feel that he was too tough on this employee in certain areas or that he was just fulfilling the responsibilities of his job by addressing the areas in the manner he chose. Think about this as you answer the following questions regarding the performance feedback meeting.

1. How do you feel this supervisor handled the performance evaluation meeting with Gene?

2. Do you agree with Gene that the Supervisor was too tough on him?

3. Do you think the supervisor held Gene responsible for things that he really couldn't control?

4. Do you think it was fair to rate Gene as "Meeting Requirements" in many of the performance areas, but make critical remarks in the comments section

of the evaluation form? Do you think that the supervisor gave Gene "mixed messages," meaning that he said he thought he was performing acceptably in certain areas, but at the same time was critical of his performance in these areas? What do you think is the danger of doing this?

5. What if the supervisor didn't address some of these issues, such as those in the Quality, Productivity, and Communications sections of the evaluation? Would Gene be aware of those aspects of his performance that his supervisor wanted to see improvement in, even though overall those areas were rated as "Meeting Requirements?"

6. Do you think that Gene made a good point about missing a few more days this past year than usual? Do you think that the supervisor should have probed more into the reason for these absences to better understand why they occurred? Do you think that the supervisor should have considered Gene's overall attendance record over the past few years, as suggested, rather than just the past year?

7. Do you think that Gene will positively resolve the communications issues he has been having with some of his co-workers? Do you think that the supervisor should have asked him more specifically how he planned on addressing these issues?

8. How likely do you think it would be that Gene becomes involved in some of the work teams, as the supervisor suggested?

9. Do you think that Gene will improve in these areas as a result of the performance feedback received during this meeting?

10. What would you have done differently if you were sitting down with this employee to review his performance based on the information you have been provides?

Chapter Review

1. What has been your greatest challenge when providing performance feedback to middle performers?

2. How can you better determine whether or not an employee is doing things right, versus doing the right things when supervising middle performers? Why do you think that making a distinction between the two activities is important? Once identified, how should you correct this situation?

3. Think of someone you have known during your career who you believe was a great communicator with others at work. What made this person effective as a communicator? What can you learn, and possibly emulate, from great communicators?

Top Performer Feedback Tips

- If you do identify someone who is focusing too much on their favorite job duties, allow this person to continue to perform these tasks; making sure that they are not being performed at the expense of other more critical duties of the position. Discuss finding a balance with this person, emphasizing why the critical tasks are important and need to be completed.

- Be careful not to discourage middle performers who are striving to be considered top performers. Provide these individuals with specific feedback on what they would need to do to be rated at a higher performance level, and support them as they strive to reach this goal.

Action Planner

During performance feedback meetings, plan on discussing what you feel is most important in the jobs that your employees perform, and compare this to what they feel is most important. Find areas of common agreement between these perceptions and encourage employees to focus particularly on those areas.

— 5 —

Dealing with Poor Performance

M any supervisors and managers struggle when dealing with poor performers. These employees are often the most challenging to manage and the ones that managers and supervisors get frustrated with the most. However, there are a number of different strategies you can employ for dealing with this level of performance, which will be covered in this chapter.

First, it is important to be able to identify what constitutes poor performance. The following are key indicators of poor or low performance:

- The first indicator is that the employee is not meeting performance expectations. These expectations should be in alignment with the business deliverables of his or her job. These should be clear and measurable.

- They are not meeting the requirements of the job. The job fulfills certain needs of the company. This is why the job exists. It is expected that the employee will deliver, as part of the responsibilities of the job. If a person is not meeting these basic requirements, this is a problem and something that should be addressed. Each member of a group, department, organization, etc. has certain goals which must be met, many of which are shared with others. If an employee is not contributing to these goals, this too must be addressed and corrected.

- In certain circumstances, low performers might disrupt others or the organization as a whole. This could be due to interpersonal relationship issues, failure to perform aspects of the job critical to others, or other reasons.

- Low performers often take up more time than other employees on non-value added issues. Dealing with issues they create ends up taking away from other, more important tasks. The 80/20 rule may be true— you end up spending 80% of your supervisory time on 20% or less of those you supervise who are poor performers.

- Low or poor performers may be subject to discipline based on their behaviors or lack of meeting their job requirements. This could be in the form of warnings about the need to improve unacceptable job performance, creating Performance Improvement Plans, or being placed on probation for poor performance, which ultimately could result in termination.

So what should you do about addressing the poor performers in your organization? There is a big difference between what you expect these employees to accomplish and what they are actually delivering, and this performance gap must be addressed. Your choices concerning dealing with poor performance are:

- Take no action and allow the poor performance to continue.

- Threaten to do something about it, while actually doing very little or nothing about it.

- Take action to address the poor performance.

Consistency is Important

Obviously, taking action to address poor performance is the best choice, but unfortunately this is not always the path that is followed. It is important that you hold everyone within the workgroup to the same performance standards concerning their jobs. Poor performers should not be allowed to lower the standards, but this is not always easy to do. In some ways, it might be easier to allow poor performance to continue, but this doesn't do anything to correct the problem. There may be a number of seemingly legitimate reasons for not addressing poor performance. A supervisor might have tried unsuccessfully in the past to take some kind of corrective action and may now feel that to continue pursuing this problem would be fruitless and a waste of their time. The supervisor may also have felt that their attempts to address poor performance were not supported by the organization.

Perhaps even worse than ignoring the problem is threatening to take some kind of corrective action but not following through with the action. Think about the message that this actually sends to a poorly-performing employee—that he or she can continue to perform at the undesirable level without any real consequence. All the employee needs to do is wait for these threatened actions to pass and then continue performing their job in the same manner.

However, you might find that before taking action to address poor performance, it is necessary to first understand what is contributing to or causing the problem. Without this understanding, you might try to apply solutions to the problem that do not really address the true cause of the problem.

The following are some of the most likely causes of poor performance:

- **Job fit.** Sometimes, the reason why an employee performs poorly is simply that the job is not a good fit for the employee (and vice versa). Some people just don't have the skills or temperament needed to perform well on certain jobs. Sometimes you need to take a step back and ask if the person is simply in the wrong job; one that doesn't match their skills. In some cases, the employee does have the potential to perform another job in the organization, if one is available. In this case, a transfer might be the best course of action.

- **Ability.** Similar to job fit, some people simply just don't have the ability to perform the job, no matter how much training and coaching they receive from their supervisor or manager. Again, in this case, helping the employee find another job opportunity, either within or outside of the organization, might be the best course of action.

- **Motivation.** In this case, the employee has the ability to perform the job, but is not motivated to do so. This is often the case when dealing with poor performers. It is also likely that at one time this employee did perform the job at an acceptable or even higher level, but at some point, lost his or her motivation to continue to perform acceptably. If this is the case, trying to determine why this individual lost his or her motivation and helping to correct the problem can be worthwhile. Sometimes, finding that one key to motivating someone can make a huge difference in his or her performance.

- **Training.** In some cases, the employee simply hasn't received the training necessary to perform the job at an acceptable level. It really isn't fair to expect someone to perform a job he or she hasn't been properly trained to perform. You need to make sure that all of your employees have been provided with the necessary training they need to perform their jobs successfully.

- **The job.** The job itself might be too demanding or too big to expect the employee to be able to perform in an acceptable manner. Sometimes with job reductions and consolidations, a job can be created that, in its scope, is nearly impossible to perform. Sometimes these changes occur over time and go unnoticed to supervisors. Make sure that the jobs you supervise are reasonable in their expectations and that you aren't asking more from employees than they can realistically deliver.

- **Supervision.** How the job is being supervised might also be a contributing factor to poor performance. Perhaps the employee may not be receiving the guidance or coaching needed, being over- or under-supervised, or there could be an existing interpersonal problem. Sometimes you need to take an honest interpersonal look to see if you are part of the problem, and consider ways in which this might be addressed.

Going back to the first two bullet items on the list of possible reasons for poor performance, you need to determine if the reason for poor job performance is a matter of ability or of motivation. There is a big difference between the two. If the employee doesn't have the prerequisite skills and ability needed to perform the job, there might not be much you can do to improve their performance. If it is a matter of ability or one of motivation, then it may be a different story, and you might be able to have an impact on improving this person's performance.

You need to ask yourself: Does the employee have the ability to perform the job at an acceptable level? Is poor performance the result of a lack of ability, or a lack of motivation? A good way to determine this is to ask yourself, if the low performer's job was on the line, would it make a difference if he or she were assigned a Performance Improvement Plan or placed on disciplinary probation, with consequences attached if tasks are not completed successfully? (The topic of Performance Improvement Plans will be covered in more detail in the next chapter.)

Sometimes putting an employee's job on the line in such a manner provides the "wake up call" he or she needs to put forth the effort needed to meet the requirements of the job. If, under this pressure, the employee is still not able to perform the job, then there is no reason to spend resources trying to improve their performance, and you should seek the help of your Human Resource Department in finding the best way to address the situation. This could include trying to help the employee find other employment that would be more suitable, either within or outside the organization.

Dealing with Poor Performance Challenges

Poor performers typically challenge you on the facts concerning their performance. They tend to place blame on others or "the system" and usually won't accept responsibility for their own poor performance. This is why it is important to be prepared with specific examples and documentation of their poor performance, if needed, to justify any consequences there may be to the individual if this performance level continues in the future. It is also important that any corrective actions planned to address these performance issues become the responsibility of the employee to complete, not the supervisor. Sometimes supervisors want to help poor performers improve their performance so much that they do everything they can to help optimize that employee's chance of improving, only to find that in trying to correct the situation, they are doing most of the work. It is fine for a supervisor to give support and provide guidance to the employee, but ultimately the employee must be committed and responsible for improving their performance to an acceptable level.

It is best to keep performance improvement discussions "behavior based," meaning that focus should only be on the specific behaviors you want the employee to change or address. If the employee can visualize what they are expected to do, they can make changes in their behavior. Telling someone that they need to change their attitude or improve their working relationships is too vague. For example, giving someone nonspecific feedback such as "you need to improve your attitude" or "you need to improve your relationships with coworkers" doesn't tell the employee what behavior is expected of them, or how their behaviors need to change. It is more effective to set specific expectations and measurable goals that are behavior-based, such as requiring the employee to:

- Participate in departmental meetings by offering constructive suggestions and opinions relevant to the discussions taking place.

- Stop interrupting others while they are speaking.

- Stop making negative comments about other employees.

- Provide assistance to others during group projects.

By providing specific examples of the changes you expect to see the employee make, there should be no confusion about what you expect from that individual in the future.

Avoid Contradictory Employment Actions

When dealing with an employee's poor job performance, allowing contradictory employment-related actions to occur only serves to confuse the situation. For example, giving an annual performance merit raise to a problem employee will weaken your argument that this person needs to change or improve their performance. The same is also true of transferring such an employee to another position, unless there is an issue with job fit and the purpose of this action is to find a more suitable position. The worst thing to do is transfer a poorly-performing employee to another position simply to be rid of them. As crazy as this may sound, this is something that does occur in many cases, for any number of reasons. You wouldn't want another supervisor transferring or promoting a problem employee into your organization, and you shouldn't do this to anyone else. You need to accept the challenge of dealing with poor performers in your workgroup yourself.

A supervisor should always expect good to excellent performance from those employees he or she supervisors. To allow poor performance to go unaddressed or challenged isn't fair to other employees who are working hard to meet or exceed the requirements of the job, especially if they are receiving the same level of compensation as those poor performers, whose work is not comparable to theirs. Financial inequity can create moral as well as motivational problems for your better performing employees.

The following is a case study involving a poorly performing employee.

CASE STUDY: POOR PERFORMER

Sandy Olsen is a highly-skilled employee, but one who has had an attitude problem about his job for most of the 15 years he has worked for the company. Sandy does exactly what he is told to do, but seldom anything more. So far, he has been able to get away with this because of his skills and abilities. There is no duty or problem that he can't handle, but seldom does he put forth any extra effort in performing his overall job. This makes supervising Sandy extremely difficult, and the instructions given to him must be very precise or the job won't get done correctly. In fact, this has infuriated all of his past supervisors over the years. Sandy's new supervisor is determined to try to get him to accept more responsibility and accountability for the job, as it is clear that he has the ability and experience to perform at a higher level than he currently does.

In preparing for today's performance evaluation, Sandy's supervisor reviewed his personnel file and found that a number of his past supervisors tried to get Sandy to perform better using disciplinary action. However, they had limited or no success. Sandy's new supervisor is wondering just how to address this problem in today's performance evaluation meeting or whether or not there really is any way to get Sandy to perform at a more acceptable level. The supervisor is considering whether or not disciplinary action should be taken to try to get Sandy's attention concerning this problem, or if there might be some other more positive way to motivate Sandy to do a better job in the future.

The supervisor is going to present Sandy with the following completed Performance Evaluation document during this meeting.

Performance Evaluation

Employee's Name: Sandy Olsen

Position: Technician

Date of Evaluation: January 6, 20____

Ratings:

- **Unacceptable:** This is a level of performance that is unacceptable and should not be allowed to continue. Immediate action is needed to address this problem performance.

- **Needs Improvement:** This level of performance needs to be improved and should not be allowed to continue in the future. A plan should be put in place to improve this level of performance to an acceptable level.

- **Meets Requirements:** This is a fully acceptable level of performance. Employees can continue at this performance level throughout their careers.

- **Exceeds Requirements:** This performance level goes beyond what is expected and exceeds the requirements of the job.

- **Exceptional:** This performance level is clearly at the highest level, going well beyond what is required or expected.

SAFETY: Performs the job safely at all times, complies with all safety requirements, wears all protective safety equipment required for the position, follows proper safe work procedures.

Safety Rating:

- ☐ Unacceptable
- ☐ Needs Improvement
- ☒ Meets Requirements
- ☐ Exceeds Requirements
- ☐ Exceptional

Comments: Sandy follows the safety requirements of his job.

QUALITY: Performs job in a quality manner, follows all required procedures, meets standards at all times, checks quality frequently, understands quality specifications and requirements of each task performed.

Quality Rating:

- ☐ Unacceptable
- ☐ Needs Improvement
- ☒ Meets Requirements
- ☐ Exceeds Requirements
- ☐ Exceptional

Comments: Sandy does basically meet the quality requirements of his position, but typically just barely. Sandy clearly understands what these requirements are and appears many times to deliberately meet only the basic requirements of a job or task.

PRODUCTIVITY: Meets productivity goals, keeps pace with work, overcomes obstacles to efficient operations, seeks ways to increase productivity, minimizes downtime, and proactively prevents slowdowns to process interruptions.

Quality Rating:

- ☐ Unacceptable
- ☒ Needs Improvement
- ☐ Meets Requirements
- ☐ Exceeds Requirements
- ☐ Exceptional

Comments: Sometimes when I assign Sandy a job or task it appears he is not working on it as quickly as possible and deliberately works slower than necessary.

COMMUNICATIONS: Shares ideas and feelings with others in a positive manner, is open to suggestions and constructive feedback, provides constructive feedback to others, is able to communicate effectively with different levels of employees in the organization, is willing to express himself in front of others including during meetings.

Communications Rating:

- ☒ Unacceptable
- ☐ Needs Improvement
- ☐ Meets Requirements
- ☐ Exceeds Requirements
- ☐ Exceptional

Comments: Again, Sandy appears to share only the minimum information about tasks that he is performing with others, including supervision. Sandy will answer questions in an accurate manner, but others must continue to probe to get all of the information from Sandy needed for them to perform their jobs correctly.

TEAMWORK: Works well with others, assists others in performing their jobs, is willing to help others deal with problems interfering with productivity, deals with conflict in a positive manner, works toward the goals of the team.

Communications Rating:

- ☒ Unacceptable
- ☐ Needs Improvement
- ☐ Meets Requirements
- ☐ Exceeds Requirements
- ☐ Exceptional

Comments: Sandy is not a team player. He prefers to work alone, where he seems to do his best work. When required to work with others, there are often complaints from coworkers about Sandy not working as a member of the team. Sandy does not respond to others' requests in a positive manner, but does do what is requested of him. Sandy's interactions with others are not always positive.

RELIABILITY: Regularly comes to work on time, can be depended upon to consistently perform at an acceptable or better level, consistently produces quality work, responds in a consistent and positive manner in all situations, has positive interactions with others on a regular basis.

Reliability Rating:

- ☐ Unacceptable
- ☐ Needs Improvement
- ☒ Meets Requirements
- ☐ Exceeds Requirements
- ☐ Exceptional

Comments: Sandy is usually reliable and meets requirements in this area, but only minimally. Sandy will get the work done, but usually on his terms with regard to how and when the work gets done.

COOPERATION: Contributes ideas to improve workplace and process on a regular basis, contributes to the team's overall efforts, makes an effort to ensure that requirements are met, especially those that directly impact the customer, consistently makes positive contributions to the team. Works positively with everyone on the team. Is willing to do what others ask and provide assistance when needed. Supports the goals and objectives of the team and the entire organization.

Cooperation Rating:

- ☒ Unacceptable
- ☐ Needs Improvement
- ☐ Meets Requirements
- ☐ Exceeds Requirements
- ☐ Exceptional

Comments: Sandy does not contribute his ideas to improve the workplace even though it is apparent to everyone who knows him that he could contribute at a significant amount.

OVERALL PERFORMANCE RATING COMMENTS:

Sandy has the talent, experience, and ability to perform his job at a much higher level than he currently performs. As Sandy's new supervisor, I am very interested in finding ways to motivate him to perform closer to this level, and ask for his feedback to help determine how this might be possible during the upcoming year. If there is no immediate improvement in Sandy's performance, further disciplinary actions will be taken to address the problem, as his current performance level cannot be allowed to continue.

The following is the discussion between the Supervisor and Sandy during their most recent annual performance feedback session.

Supervisor: Sandy, come on in and have a seat. Today I want to review your annual performance evaluation. Even though I'm relatively new to this position, there are a number of things that I've observed concerning your overall performance that I want to discuss with you today.

Sandy: How long is this going to take? I have a lot of things that I need to take care of this afternoon.

Supervisor: We're going to discuss your performance for a while this afternoon. I have covered your position for the time we are together, so don't worry about it for now. What I have to discuss with you today is very important, so I want to make sure that I have your full attention while we talk. Okay?

Sandy: Yeah, okay, but I think this is just a waste of time. Nothing ever comes out of these meetings anyways.

Supervisor: Well, as your new supervisor, I am hoping that this meeting is going to be different.

Sandy: We'll see.

Supervisor: Well, let's get started. The first area I want to discuss is Safety. I rated you as "Meets Requirements" in this area. I have observed that you do generally follow the safety requirements of the job, and that is good.

Sandy:	I work around some dangerous equipment and I don't want to get hurt doing it!
Supervisor:	I certainly agree and support your continued attention to the safety requirements of the job. The next area I want to discuss is Quality. I did rate you as "Meets Requirements" in this area; however, I struggled with giving you this high a rating. As I said in my comments, you do basically meet the quality requirements of the job, but just barely.
Sandy:	What's the problem, then, if I'm meeting the quality requirements?
Supervisor:	The problem is that I know you can do better. There are times when it seems that you deliberately do only the minimum, when you are fully capable of doing better. What do you have to say about this?
Sandy:	Again, I don't see why this is a problem. I always do exactly what I'm asked to do.
Supervisor:	Yes, but that's the problem. What I want you to do is your best work, not the minimum to get by. Sometimes the person asking for your help doesn't know what to do to address a problem. Because of your experience and ability, you are in a better position to know what needs to be done to improve our operations and ultimately serve the customer. I am not going to let this go. This is something that I want to see you change in the future. We will be talking more about this as we go through this evaluation.

	Now let's move on to Productivity. I rated you as "Needs Improvement" in this area. I rated you at this lower level because I believe that you can work faster to complete assignments than you presently do. Your response and completion times are the lowest in our workgroup. This is not acceptable and needs to change.
Sandy:	This is what I don't understand. On the one hand you are saying that you want me to do a higher quality job, and now you're telling me that I should be working faster. I think you need to make up your mind as to what you really want from me!
Supervisor:	You and I both know that you can do a better job in both of these areas if you wanted to, without sacrificing one for the other.
Sandy:	I don't agree. I'm just trying to do what's asked of me on the job.
Supervisor:	I don't buy that and I don't really think you mean what you're saying. As I said, you are capable of doing much more than that. Again, I'm not going to let this go either. I'm going to be paying attention to your productivity numbers and discussing this with you on a regular basis going forward. I know that you can do better, and I won't be satisfied until you do.
	The next area to discuss is Communication. My comments were: *Again, Sandy appears to share only the minimum information about tasks that he is performing with others, including supervision. Sandy will answer questions in an accurate manner,*

but others must continue to probe to get all of the information from Sandy needed for them to perform their jobs correctly. This is a constant theme in this area, as you do only the minimum when it comes to sharing information, including with me. I can think of several times, including that incident last week, when just because I hadn't asked for specific information, you didn't tell me something that turned out to be important. When I questioned you about it, all you said was that I never asked about it. This isn't good enough for me. I believe you knew full well the importance of that information but choose not to share it just to make my job more difficult. This behavior can lead to bigger problems, which could be prevented by sharing information more proactively. Again, this is something that needs to change immediately.

Sandy: Like I said before, I answer everybody's questions and provide whatever information they want.

Supervisor: Alright, I already told you what I expect from you in this area. The next thing I want to talk about is Teamwork. I also rated you as Unacceptable in this area. As I said, you are not a team player. You don't contribute to team efforts and clearly prefer to work by yourself. Your coworkers don't like working with you and would prefer that they not have to work with you. This is not acceptable or consistent with my operating philosophy of teamwork and is not the best use of our resources.

Sandy: Why don't others want to work with me? I always pull my own weight and do my share of the work.

Supervisor: It's not just an issue of pulling your own weight. You are perfectly capable of doing that. The complaints I get about you are in regard to the way you treat others. You are usually not responsive to anything they say to you and you always act like you know more than them on just about everything. You don't listen to their suggestions and just do things you own way. Granted, I will give you that you probably do know more than most of the others in the group, but there certainly are more positive ways you could deal with your coworkers.

Sandy: What do you want me to do? If their suggestions are wrong, or not the most efficient way of doing things, should I just let them make mistakes and cause further problems?

Supervisor: No, I wouldn't want you to do that either. But what I would like you to do is to help your co-workers learn from your experience and expertise. Help them find better ways to do the job, not just push them away and do it your own way. You need to at least listen and consider their ideas and what they have to say.

Okay, let's move on to Reliability. I did rate you as "Meets Requirements" in this area although again only minimally. As we have already discussed, you do get things done, but you do it on your own terms rather than anyone else's.

Sandy:	So what's the problem?
Supervisor:	This is an area where you just get by because of your skills and knowledge. You might get the job done, but it's not always the best way of doing things. As I've already explained, we can achieve much more working together as a team than as individuals working separately.
	The last area is Cooperation and I rated you as lowest in this area. You don't contribute to the team's overall efforts and this hurts our ability to serve our customers. Also, you don't work positively with others. Again, this is something that has to change immediately. Do you have anything you want to say about this rating?
Sandy:	No, I can see that it won't do any good anyway. This is no different than my other evaluations from all the other supervisors I have worked for before. You are just trying to find ways to criticize me so you can promote your other favorite employees who do everything you say.
Supervisor:	I am sorry you feel this way, but I need to tell you that I don't play favorites with any employees. I just want everyone, including you, to do their best on their jobs to help contribute to our group's overall goals.
	Finally, I want to review your overall rating. I also gave you the lowest rating of "Unacceptable." I am going to read my overall comments:
	Sandy has the talent, experience, and ability to perform his job at a much higher level than he currently performs. As Sandy's new

supervisor, I am very interested in finding ways to motivate him to perform closer to this level, and I ask for his feedback to help determine how this might be possible during the upcoming year. If there is no immediate improvement in Sandy's performance, further disciplinary actions will be taken to address this problem, as this current performance level cannot be allowed to continue.

I think this says it all concerning how I feel about your performance. I can't just sit by and allow you to continue to not perform to your ability. I am not sure what is going on with you, and why you have this negative attitude about the job. If you don't do something to change, I am afraid that there are going to be some negative consequences for you.

Sandy: Hey, I've been through all this before with my other supervisors. I know my rights concerning how I should be treated as an employee. You have no right to score me that low when I'm doing the job correctly and you think I should be doing better. I've heard all that "teamwork" talk many times over the years, and it's nothing but a waste of time. What we need is someone who knows what they are doing, and that someone is me. All you have to do is go to Human Resources and have them tell you how it is. In fact, I'm going to go to them right after work this afternoon to tell them about this unfair evaluation, and they will take care of it.

Supervisor: Well, you are certainly welcome to go and talk to them. But you should also know that I reviewed this situation with our Human Resources department, and that they are supportive of these actions. But that isn't what I really want to see happen here, and I'm sure you don't either. What I really want to learn from our meeting today is why you are so unmotivated by your job. Clearly you are the most experienced and talented person in our group, yet you only do the minimum required on your job. I am new to this role, and I don't know all of the history that took place before I came to this area, and I don't really have a clue about why you feel the way you do. Can you give me some idea what this is all about?

Sandy: Well, when I first started working here, I used to try to do more, but it never got me anywhere. My supervisors would tell me that if I continued to work hard I would get promoted and make a lot more money, but that never happened. They all just took credit for what I did to get themselves promoted. It was really only about how *they* could benefit from *my* hard work, not what I could get out of it.

Supervisor: I appreciate you sharing this with me and I'm beginning to understand why you feel the way you do about your job. I can't change what happened in the past, but I can have an influence on what we do going forward. Can you share with me what you would like to see done differently?

Sandy: Well for one thing, I would like to make sure that I get recognized for what I do on the job, rather than have others steal the credit.

Supervisor: Okay, how would you like this recognition to look?

Sandy: Well, I'd like to have you, as my supervisor, acknowledge what I do and what I've accomplished. This never happened in the past.

Supervisor: Okay, fair enough. Is there anything else you would like to see happen differently?

Sandy: Well, I'm still interested in moving ahead in my job somehow. I have been doing the same thing for many years now, and there aren't many challenges for me anymore in this job.

Supervisor: There are a number of things that we could do to help this happen. For one thing, as I mentioned earlier, you could help some of the newer employees learn from your experience. But first you need to pay attention to the things we discussed today. It is important that I, as well as others in the organization, perceive your attitude about your work differently. I think that this is entirely possible, and there are things you can surely do. I'm willing to help you as much as I can to change this situation, but ultimately it is your responsibility to make these changes.

Sandy: Well, I'll have to see if you really mean it or not. Like I said, I've heard all this before.

Supervisor: Okay, that's fair. I can tell you, I'm very interested in helping you improve your job performance and would like to see you reach your full potential. I feel that this is one of the most important responsibilities I have as a supervisor, and that I wouldn't be doing my job if I didn't try to help all of those who reported to me to develop on their jobs and reach their career goals.

Let's end this meeting now, as we are out of time. But let's meet on a regular basis to discuss what we can do to help you become more interested and motivated on your job. We'll see what happens from there. Does that sound alright?

Sandy: Yeah, I guess so.

Supervisor: Okay, I'll get in touch with you soon to follow up on our discussion today and begin looking at things we can do to help you in the future.

Performance Feedback Evaluation Meeting Debrief

Given the potential of this employee, the current performance level being demonstrated is clearly not acceptable. The supervisor makes this clear during the discussion, and lets the employee know that something has to change to avoid negative consequences to the employee's career with this company. The following questions further emphasize how the supervisor dealt with this problem. Think about the likelihood of this employee changing his behavior in the future, and whether or not the supervisor really did get him to take his situation seriously.

1. How well do you think the supervisor handled this performance evaluation?

2. Do you think that the supervisor addressed the employee's performance problems correctly?

3. Do you think that the supervisor rated this employee too harshly on some of the performance areas given, and that the employee was actually meeting the basic requirements in those performance areas?

4. How justified do you feel Sandy is in his feelings and attitude towards his job?

5. Why do you think that it is important to understand why the people who work for you feel the way they do? How can this help you to address their issues? How well do you think this supervisor did in trying to get a better understanding of what contributed to Sandy's attitude towards his job?

6. Do you think that it was a good idea for this supervisor to seek advice and support from the Human Resource Department before presenting this evaluation to Sandy? Why or why not?

7. Do you think that the supervisor emphasized enough to this employee what the consequences would be if he didn't change his behaviors going forward?

8. Do you think that if the employee doesn't improve there will be the negative consequences that the supervisor said could happen?

9. What if Sandy doesn't change and there are no negative consequences? What does this actually say to the employee?

10. The supervisor tried to end meeting on a positive note, saying that he would set up a time for the two of them to continue their discussion on how to motivate this employee in the future. Do you think at this point the supervisor should have re-emphasized, more strongly, the consequences to the employee if he doesn't change his attitude? Why or why not?

Chapter Review

1. What is the biggest challenge for you when dealing with poor performance in your workgroup?

2. Think about a time when you had to deal with an employee's poor performance. What do you think was the cause of this problem? Was the problem a matter of ability, or of motivation?

3. How can having a better understanding of the cause of performance problems help you better understand how to most effectively deal with them?

Top Performer Feedback Tips

- Make sure that you document the employee's poor performance, as well as make notes of all meetings you have with the employee to help correct the poor performance.

- Try to find positive ways to address poor performance, especially matters concerning the employee's motivation.

- Consult with your Human Resources Department for assistance in dealing with poor performance.

Action Planner

It is very important that you follow up on every corrective action you have planned for a poor performer, in
accordance with the timetable you established for these
actions.

Set calendar reminders to alert you as to when follow-
up actions are scheduled to discuss progress toward
corrective action goals you have established for poor
performers, and keep the progress moving forward.

— 6 —
Performance Improvement Plans

U nfortunately, trying to coach and counsel a poorly-performing employee through the normal performance feedback processes established by the organization might not always be successful. There are situations when a more aggressive approach is necessary. Placing an employee who is performing poorly on a Performance Improvement Plan (PIP) is a clear way to send the message that his or her performance needs to improve or there will be consequences that could include termination. A Performance Improvement Plan should be part of your organization's disciplinary process, with the same consequences as for nonconformance and other infractions of the rules and policies of the organization. Discipline should always be intended to help an employee improve his or her performance and behaviors in the future, not to punish the employee. Punishment usually only serves to make someone resentful and doesn't teach what needs to be done in the future to be successful. That is why it is best to approach any discipline in a constructive manner, where an employee can have a chance to prove that he or she can be a good performer in the future.

It is important to keep in mind that a Performance Improvement Plan should only be utilized after the normal performance feedback processes described previously have failed to yield acceptable results and is typically the last step taken before termination to try to address and improve an employee's unacceptable performance.

There must be continuity between a company's formal performance feedback process and a Performance Improvement Plan. The Performance Improvement Plan should not be the first time an employee learns that he or she is not performing at an acceptable level. It should follow the coaching and counseling received during the normal performance feedback process, as was illustrated in the previous chapter. It is likely that an employee may not agree with the reasons for the performance improvement plan, and may even challenge these reasons or blame others for their own poor performance. Denial of responsibility could be the basis for the employee's performance problems in the first place. However, a Performance Improvement Plan is not a process that requires an employee's agreement. The employee was previously given the opportunity for a one-on-one discussion with their supervisor during the organization's normal performance feedback process. This is the time for the employee to listen carefully to what they need to do to improve performance, and even save their job.

Presenting a performance improvement plan to an employee is a very serious matter. If you are not prepared to carry out the provisions of the plan, then it should not be undertaken. An employee also shouldn't be placed on a performance improvement plan if there is not documentation supporting this action. You need to be able to provide specific and documented reasons and rationale for why this action is being taken. It is important that the performance improvement plan be designed to place the burden of responsibility for reaching the objectives of the plan on the employee and not the supervisor. It will not help either the employee or the supervisor if all of the work to make sure that the goals of the plan are achieved ends up being done by the supervisor.

Establishing SMART Goals

It is especially important that the goals established in a performance improvement plan are in line with "SMART" goals. SMART goals were first introduced by George T. Doran in 1981. SMART is an acronym for:

Specific—what is to be accomplished is described exactly

Measurable—levels of accomplishment are measurable and based on quality, cost, timelines, etc.

Agreed-upon—goals are agreed upon between employee and supervisor

Realistic—goals are achievable, yet challenging

Time-bound—goals have specific timetables for achievement, including end dates

This same principle, so important in your performance feedback process, also applies to a performance improvement plan. This is especially true when it comes to providing feedback and evaluating progress against performance improvement goals. Each performance goal must be able to be measured and evaluated.

The last factor of the Performance Improvement Plan format requires the supervisor to provide a rating on how the individual is performing in relation to each PIP goal, either as Acceptable, Improving, or Unacceptable. The **SMARTer** the goal, the more accurately this measurement can potentially be at the end of the process.

The following is a suggested format for a Performance Improvement Plan. It includes seven main areas of focus to be addressed by the supervisor when presenting the plan to an employee:

- Job requirements to be addressed
- Performance problems
- Performance goals
- Support
- Timeline to address performance issues
- Times for meeting and reviewing progress
- Results

Generally, it is best to limit the areas to be addressed to no more than eight in order to focus on those aspects of the employee's job performance that need the most attention.

The following is an example of a completed Performance Improvement Plan. In this case, the plan is for a customer service representative not meeting the requirements of the position as stated at the beginning of this process.

PERFORMANCE IMPROVEMENT PLAN

Name: Jan White

Dates of Plan: May 1, 20____ - July 31, 20____

Position: Customer Service Representative

Date of Meeting: April 30, 20____

Completed by Supervisor: Frank Henderson

Job Requirements to be Addressed	Performance Problem(s)	Performance Goal	Support	Time-table	Follow-up Date	RESULTS* Acceptable Unacceptable Improving
Understand the needs of the customer	Not calling on right customers/ spending too much time and money on wrong customers	Create list of top 20 customers in territory	Work with Regional Sales Manager	Due May 7	May 7	TBD
Planning and organization	Missing appointments; not following up with customers and deadlines	Create and submit within 7 days: Monthly visit schedule for each account by phone or in person	Utilize top 20 list Review plan with Regional Sales Manager by 3rd day of month	Due May 7	May 7	TBD

Job Requirements to be Addressed	Performance Problem(s)	Performance Goal	Support	Time-table	Follow-up Date	RESULTS* Acceptable Unacceptable Improving
Planning and organization (continued)		Continued... Make appts. with each customer at least 1 week in advance In the future, submit plan to supervisor by end of month				
Reliability	Lack of confidence others have in your dependability— too many missed deadlines and unmet commitments.	Respond to all customer inquiries, complaints, issues, requests, etc. within two business days.	Regional Sales Manager R&D Tech Services Distribution	Immed.	May 14	TBD

Job Requirements to be Addressed	Performance Problem(s)	Performance Goal	Support	Time-table	Follow-up Date	RESULTS* Acceptable Unacceptable Improving
Reliability (continued)		Continued... Ensure all follow-ups completed 100% Inform supervisor of all such contracts				
Communications	Failure to keep supervisor informed on critical information relating to accounts	Eliminate surprises to supervisor concerning customer issues. Call/email supervisor at least 3 times/week with customer contact communications	Supervisor Help Desk VMX Support	Immed.	May 14	TBD

Job Requirements to be Addressed	Performance Problem(s)	Performance Goal	Support	Time-table	Follow-up Date	RESULTS* Acceptable Unacceptable Improving
Communications (continued)		Respond to all VMX's/emails within 24 hours				

All performance areas included in this Performance Improvement Plan must reach an *Acceptable* result level by the end of the performance plan period. If, at the end of the plan, there remain performance factors not at an Acceptable performance level, employee's employment will be terminated.

Attach any documentation as needed or appropriate to support the Performance Improvement Plan.

As part of the presentation, it is suggested that a cover letter to the Performance Improvement Plan be presented to the employee and reviewed. This letter explains what will be expected of the employee during the Performance Improvement Plan period that has been established, and that continued improvement is also expected. The letter informs the employee that if at any time during the plan period he or she is not showing adequate improvement, the plan can be ended and his or her employment terminated. The cover letter also explains that simply getting through the plan isn't enough and that once this level of acceptable performance is achieved it is expected to be maintained by the employee. When someone successfully completes a Performance Improvement Plan, he or she has shown that the problem is not in ability, but in some other factor. The point that is being emphasized is that establishing and monitoring a Performance Improvement Plan is a very labor extensive process for the supervisor or manager and others involved, and is not something that the company is willing to do more than once for an employee. The company cannot continually keep trying to motivate an employee to perform their job at an acceptable level if the employee is not motivated to do this.

The following is an example of a format for such a letter:

To:

Re: Performance Improvement Plan

Date:

The purpose of this letter is to serve as notification that you are being placed on a 90-day Performance Improvement Plan as your performance continues to fall below acceptable levels.

We have developed a performance improvement plan that outlines what will be expected of you during this period. It is attached for your review and follow-up. The performance improvement plan covers, in detail, the following items:

- Requirements of the job not presently being met
- Problems with your current performance
- Goals for improvement of your performance
- Support that will be provided to you
- The timeline established for you to address performance issues
- Times that we will meet and review your progress
- The expected performance and measurement criteria

If your performance is still unacceptable at any point going through this performance plan, you will be discharged. Your performance must continue to meet or exceed all acceptable levels. Upon successful completion of this plan, you will be expected to maintain the desired level of performance on each of these success factors in the future. You will not be given another Performance Improvement Plan. Instead, future unacceptable performance will result in termination of your employment.

It is my sincere hope that you will reach these acceptable performance levels and demonstrate that you can work as a contributing and successful part of our team.

I will be available to help you achieve the goals of this Performance Improvement Plan. However, it is also important for you to realize that you must accept primary responsibility for the success of this plan. Please contact me should you have any questions about this plan.

Sincerely,

Supervisor

It is important that a supervisor does everything he or she commits to doing as part of this process, especially concerning follow-up meetings. Failure on the part of the supervisor in meeting his or her commitments could negate the entire Performance Improvement Plan process. But also, as emphasized in this cover letter, it is important that the employee assume primary responsibility for his or her improvement during the process.

A Performance Improvement Plan needs to be linked to other processes to ensure consistency. It is important that there be a link to the employee's performance feedback evaluation document if only to reference the fact that a Performance Improvement Plan is or has been in effect during the performance evaluation period. Subsequently, other appropriate personnel-related actions should be consistent with this level of performance. Consideration should be given concerning the amount (if any) of salary increases that someone who is on a Performance Improvement Plan should receive, the ratings that person receives, eligibility for job transfers, consideration and talent review ratings. The most important point is that there should be consistency between all of these personnel-related actions. Otherwise, this creates confusion and inconsistent management of an employee's poor performance.

The ultimate goal of a Performance Improvement Plan should be for the employee to complete the plan successfully and then receive future performance feedback via the organization's established performance feedback process. Also, the normal performance feedback meetings should continue to take place even when a Performance Improvement Plan is actively in place for continuity to be maintained.

There are a number of benefits to engaging in a Performance Improvement Process. It documents specifically the employee's poor performance and shows how the supervisor attempted to help address the issue. It eliminates the excuse many employees have that no one ever told them that they were not performing at an unacceptable level, or what was expected of them, or that it helps create a legal defense to support a potential termination if the Performance Improvement Plan is not ultimately successful.

Finally, it is a fair process. It tells the employee specifically what performance areas are unacceptable, what he or she needs to do to improve the poor performance, what support will be provided to help the employee improve, and how performance will be measured. It also explains the consequences of not successfully completing the plan, as well as what will be expected of the employee in the future if the plan is completed successfully.

Documentation is also important in the performance management process. Good documentation creates a "historical snapshot" of what has previously occurred relating to an employee's performance. Poor performance should be documented to help provide the justification for poor performance ratings. Documenting poor performance validates and creates a written justification for such actions as well as a legal defense should one be needed at a later date. Documentation should be consistent and supportive of any actions that are recommended, and will be the basis of any decisions or approval of employment actions requested for review. When creating documentation, it is important to follow the 5W's:

- **Who**—think about who will see this documentation. For purposes of performance management, you should create documentation with the thought that it very well may end up being reviewed by someone outside of the company, such as a government regulatory agency, an arbitrator, an attorney, a judge, or even a jury.

- **What**—think about what you would want someone else to know about this employment action, as well as the circumstances behind it. Keep your documentation to the point and only include information and facts pertinent to the actions you are taking. Creating too much or unnecessary documentation should be avoided.

- **When**—creating an accurate timeline of events or recording the times and dates that certain critical actions occurred helps to explain the sequence of events that led to the actions taken. It is important to keep employment actions consistent with current events, not based on past or out-of-date performance.

- **Where**—For documentation to be clear, it should explain where the events occurred that support the actions being taken. There should be no question where certain events or circumstances leading up to the employment action took place.

- **Why**—It is important to document precisely why certain employment actions were taken, as well as the justification for these actions. In other words, there should be a clear explanation for each action.

It is also important to understand that there are certain legal implications when creating documentation. This document can be discoverable in a legal proceeding and ordered to be submitted to a third party or legal representative of someone involved in litigation against the company. Care should be taken to include only factual information in any electronic documentation you might create. Opinions, suspicions, and jokes related to the event should never be included in this type of documentation. Again, keep in mind when writing documentation that it could be used as part of a legal proceeding at a later date and viewed by third parties outside the company. Seek further guidance on this subject from your human resources or legal departments.

Constructive Confrontation

Although confronting poor performance is not easy and usually uncomfortable, if you deal with the facts, keep it behavior based, providing descriptive examples of the problem, it usually flows much smoother and is better received. What is needed is *constructive confrontation.* This means that you are confronting the poor performer but in a developmental or constructive manner. It would be worse to do nothing about the employee's poor performance, especially if this results in adverse consequences for the employee, such as being terminated. By addressing performance issues in this manner, you are telling the employee specifically what performance areas are unacceptable, what he or she needs to do to improve their performance, what support will be provided to help improve performance, and how performance will be measured. It also explains the consequences of not successfully completing the Performance Improvement Plan, as well as what will be expected of the employee in the future if the plan is completed successfully.

The goal should always be to help the employee improve their performance to an acceptable or better level. This results in a win/win scenario in which both the employee and the company benefit. However, you might not always be able to achieve this result. Sometimes, despite a manager's or supervisor's best efforts to help an employee improve his or her performance, this goal is not achieved.

In either case, you have at least addressed the poor performance and brought the issue to some kind of resolution. This is much better than simply ignoring poor performance or just tolerating it without taking any action to address the problem. If a supervisor or manager does a good job managing poor performance, one of two things will happen:

- The goal will be achieved. The performance will be improved and there will be a win/win result.

- The manager or supervisor will have helped justify and support the need for future discipline and/or termination. In this case, the supervisor has at least created a stronger justification for any adverse employment actions that might now need to be taken.

— 7 —
Helping Employees Climb the Career Ladder

Regardless of their performance level, one of the most important responsibilities you have towards all of your employees is to help them grow and develop in their careers. The following are ways in which you can help your employees climb the career ladder.

- **Encourage employees to learn new skills and add value to their position.** Employees want to learn new skills on the job, as this makes them more valuable to the company and helps them continue to grow and develop.

- **Help develop a strategy for success.** As a manager or supervisor, you need to help develop a strategy for employees to be successful in their careers. This includes addressing any developmental or training needs that can help the employee continue to progress in his or her career.

- **Encourage employees to seek support from others (mentors).** Encourage employees to seek help and support from others in the organization by either assigning a mentor or encouraging employees to seek mentors on their own.

- **Let others in the organization know their career goals.** As a supervisor or manager, you have a responsibility to let others in the organization know what your employees' career goals and aspirations are so they can help make these goals eventually become realities whenever possible.

- **Help employees add value to their positions.** You should help employees understand how to add value to their positions in the organization. No matter what role they play, there are always ways to make their positions more valuable. This is one way to inspire employees to show that they are capable of accepting greater levels of responsibility in the future.

- **Help employees expect and accept change.** Finally, help employees learn to deal with and accept change. This can be one of the most important skills that anyone can acquire in the workplace today.

— Summary —

This book was designed to help you in being better able to provide formal feedback and guidance to your employees. Review the concepts presented in this book before the next performance feedback meetings with your direct reports. Commit the time and effort to the performance feedback process necessary to perform this job responsibility to the best of your ability.

It is important to remember that providing formal feedback is only part of the overall communications you need to have with those who report to you. You also need to provide feedback to your employees on a regular basis throughout the year. Providing feedback to employees can make everyone's job more fulfilling, including yours as a supervisor or manager.

— Appendix —

Non-Exempt Performance Evaluation Document

Employee's Name:

Position:

Date of Evaluation:

Ratings:

- **Unacceptable:** This is a level of performance that is unacceptable and should not be allowed to continue. Immediate action is needed to address this problem performance.

- **Needs Improvement:** This level of performance needs to be improved and should not be allowed to continue in the future. A plan should be put in place to improve this level of performance to an acceptable level.

- **Meets Requirements:** This is a fully acceptable level of performance. Employees can continue at this performance level throughout their careers.

- **Exceeds Requirements:** This performance level goes beyond what is expected and exceeds the requirements of the job.

- **Exceptional:** This performance level is clearly at the highest level, going well beyond what is required or expected.

SAFETY: Performs the job safely at all times, complies with all safety requirements, wears all protective safety equipment required for the position, follows proper safe work procedures.

Safety Rating:

- ☐ Unacceptable
- ☐ Needs Improvement
- ☐ Meets Requirements
- ☐ Exceeds Requirements
- ☐ Exceptional

Comments:

QUALITY: Performs job in a quality manner, follows all required procedures, meets standards at all times, checks quality frequently, understands quality specifications and requirements of each task performed.

Quality Rating:

- ☐ Unacceptable
- ☐ Needs Improvement
- ☐ Meets Requirements
- ☐ Exceeds Requirements
- ☐ Exceptional

Comments:

PRODUCTIVITY: Meets productivity goals, keeps pace with work, overcomes obstacles to efficient operations, seeks ways to increase productivity, minimizes downtime, and proactively prevents slowdowns to process interruptions.

Quality Rating:

- ☐ Unacceptable
- ☐ Needs Improvement
- ☐ Meets Requirements
- ☐ Exceeds Requirements
- ☐ Exceptional

Comments:

COMMUNICATIONS: Shares ideas and feelings with others in a positive manner, is open to suggestions and constructive feedback, provides constructive feedback to others, is able to communicate effectively with different levels of employees in the organization, is willing to express himself in front of others including during meetings.

Communications Rating:

- ☐ Unacceptable
- ☐ Needs Improvement
- ☐ Meets Requirements
- ☐ Exceeds Requirements
- ☐ Exceptional

Comments:

TEAMWORK: Works well with others, assists others in performing their jobs, is willing to help others deal with problems interfering with productivity, deals with conflict in a positive manner, works toward the goals of the team.

Communications Rating:

- ☐ Unacceptable
- ☐ Needs Improvement
- ☐ Meets Requirements
- ☐ Exceeds Requirements
- ☐ Exceptional

Comments:

RELIABILITY: Regularly comes to work on time, can be depended upon to consistently perform at an acceptable or better level, produce quality work, respond in a positive manner in all situations, and have positive interactions with others on a regular basis.

Reliability Rating:

- ☐ Unacceptable
- ☐ Needs Improvement
- ☐ Meets Requirements
- ☐ Exceeds Requirements
- ☐ Exceptional

Comments:

COOPERATION: Contributes ideas to improve workplace and process on a regular basis, contributes to the team's overall efforts, makes an effort to ensure that requirements are met, especially those that directly impact the customer, and consistently makes positive contributions to the team. Works positively with everyone on the team. Is willing to do what others ask and provide assistance when needed. Supports the goals and objectives of the team and the entire organization.

Cooperation Rating:

- ☐ Unacceptable
- ☐ Needs Improvement
- ☐ Meets Requirements
- ☐ Exceeds Requirements
- ☐ Exceptional

Comments:

Overall Performance Rating:

- ☐ Unacceptable
- ☐ Needs Improvement
- ☐ Meets Requirements
- ☐ Exceeds Requirements
- ☐ Exceptional

OVERALL PERFORMANCE RATING COMMENTS:

_____   _____
Supervisor Signature   Date

_____   _____
Employee Signature   Date

_____   _____
Department Manager Signature   Date

PERFORMANCE IMPROVEMENT PLAN

Name:

Dates of Plan:

Completed by Supervisor:

Position:

Date of Meeting:

Job Requirements to be Addressed	Performance Problem(s)	Performance Goal	Support	Time-table	Follow-up Date	RESULTS* Acceptable Unacceptable Improving

Job Requirements to be Addressed	Performance Problem(s)	Performance Goal	Support	Time-table	Follow-up Date	RESULTS* Acceptable Unacceptable Improving

Job Requirements to be Addressed	Performance Problem(s)	Performance Goal	Support	Time-table	Follow-up Date	RESULTS* Acceptable Unacceptable Improving

All performance areas included in this Performance Improvement Plan must reach an *Acceptable* level by the end of the performance plan period. If at the end of the plan there remain performance factors not at an Acceptable performance level, employee's employment will be terminated.

Attach any documentation as needed or appropriate to support the Performance Improvement Plan.

Manager's Performance Feedback
Self-Assessment Questions

What are some the greatest challenges you face when it comes to providing effective performance feedback to those who report to you?

What support do you feel you need to be able to do a better job providing performance feedback to your employees who work for you? How can you get this support in the future?

What level of performer do you find the most challenging to provide performance feedback for?

What can you do to make providing feedback to this level of employee more productive?

What can you do to provide better career guidance to employees that work for you?

What are some of the biggest challenges you face in trying to provide this guidance to these employees?

Who in the organization can you go to for guidance in providing better performance feedback to your employees? How well do you utilize these resources?

What other resources are available to you to help you become more effective in providing this feedback to your employees?

What do you think are the expectations of those who report to you concerning the performance feedback they receive from you?

Do you think you are meeting or exceeding these expectations? If not, what can you do to change this situation?

Do you try to connect the feedback that you give to employees during formal performance feedback evaluations with your day-to-day interactions with them?

Do you ensure that all follow-up actions discussed and agreed upon during performance feedback meetings are completed?

Do you ensure that employees are assigned accountability for at least some of these action items, and that these are followed-up by you as well?

Do you give any thought as to how to approach each employee differently based on his or her individual need for feedback?

Do you think of spending time providing performance feedback to employees as a good investment in your time, or something that you are required to do as part of your job as a manager or supervisor? How much effect do you think the difference between these two attitudes has on how your employees feel about the performance feedback they receive?

Employee Performance
Feedback Survey

Please answer the following questions concerning the performance feedback you receive from your supervisor. Circle the appropriate number that best describes your response to each question.

1. How valuable to you is the performance feedback you receive from your supervisor?

1	2	3	4	5
Not Valuable	Sometimes Valuable	Mostly Valuable	Very Valuable	Extremely Valuable

2. How accurately do you feel the performance feedback you receive from your supervisor reflects your actual job performance?

1	2	3	4	5
Not at all Accurate	Somewhat Accurate	Mostly Accurate	Very Accurate	Extremely Accurate

3. When giving feedback on your performance, how often does your supervisor provide you with positive feedback as well as discussing areas that he/she would like to see you improve?

1	2	3	4	5
Never	Rarely	Sometimes	Most of the Time	Always

4. Does your supervisor follow up on the action items discussed during performance feedback meetings?

1	2	3	4	5
Never	Rarely	Sometimes	Most of the Time	Always

5. How often do you receive career guidance from your supervisor during performance feedback evaluation meetings?

1	2	3	4	5
Never	Rarely	Sometimes	Most of the Time	Always

6. How valuable has the guidance you received from your supervisor concerning career goals been to you in helping you reach these goals?

1	2	3	4	5
Not Valuable	Sometimes Valuable	Mostly Valuable	Very Valuable	Extremely Valuable

7. How often does your supervisor meet with you to provide you with performance feedback?

1	2	3	4	5
Never	Rarely	Sometimes	Most of the Time	Always

8. How committed do you think your supervisor is to the performance feedback process?

1	2	3	4	5
Not Committed	Somewhat Committed	Fairly Committed	Committed	Very Committed

9. Do you believe that the organization is committed to the performance feedback process and encourages or requires everyone to utilize this process on a regular basis?

1	2	3	4	5
Not Committed	Somewhat Committed	Fairly Committed	Committed	Very Committed

10. What changes would you like to see happen in the organization's current performance feedback process?

_____

_____

_____

_____

_____

_____

_____

_____

_____

_____

_____

_____

_____

_____

_____

_____

_____

_____